This Book Belongs To

This book is dedicated to
My family
Wade, Logan and Carter
Without you this would not have been possible
Together we can do anything!

To my Rainbow Loom family
Choon , Fen, Teresa and Michelle
For the inspiration

To my Learning Express family
and Sharon DiMinico
for fostering the entrepreneurial spirit!

Beginner Level Photo Gallery

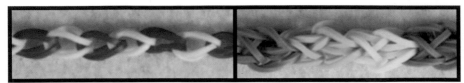

SINGLE CHAIN BRACELET   16   DIAMOND BRACELET   18

DIAMOND RIDGE BRACELET   20   HONEYCOMB BRACELET   24

SINGLE RHOMBUS BRACELET   26   TRIANGLE BRACELET   28

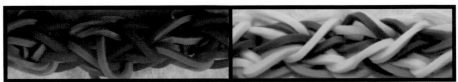

SPECKLED RHOMBUS BRACELET   30   DIAMOND TRIO BRACELET   32

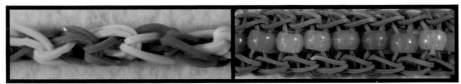

SPIRAL BRACELET   34   BEAD LADDER BRACELET   36

TRIPLE SINGLE BRACELET   38   TRIPLE SINGLE BACKPACK TAG   42

Intermediate Level Photo Gallery

TAFFY TWIST BRACELET   48   DOUBLE BEAD LADDER BRACELET 52

RAINBOW LADDER BRACELET   56   ZIPPY CHAIN BRACELET   61

HOLIDAY BRACELET   64   TEAM SPIRIT BRACELET   70

LIBERTY TWIST BRACELET   67   DOUBLE FORWARD RHOMBUS   74

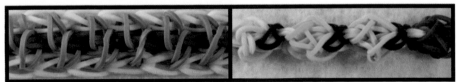

DOUBLE REARWARD RHOMBUS   76   TULIP TOWER BRACELET   78

CROSSED HEXAGON RING   80   BUTTERFLY BLOSSOM RING   82

Intermediate Level Photo Gallery

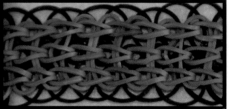

Advanced Level Photo Gallery

Zig Zag Bracelet   118

Starfish Bracelet   120

Twistzy Wistzy Bracelet   122

Ladybug Bracelet   126

Honey Bee Bracelet   128

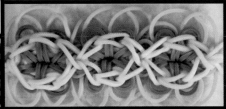

Star Burst Bracelet   132

Flower Power Bracelet   138

Rainbow Blooms Bracelet   144

Carnation Bracelet   152

Rainbow Bloom Charm   150

Advanced Level Photo Gallery

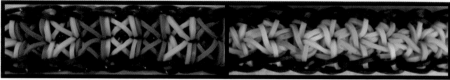

BIRD OF PARADISE BRACELET   156   DELTA WING BRACELET   160

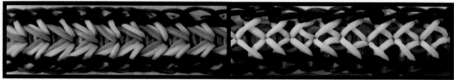

TOTEM POLE BRACELET   162   FEN'S FANTASTIC BRACELET   165

FEATHER BRACELET   168   CONFETTI CRISS-CROSS   172

HIBISCUS BRACELET   180

Table of Contents

Beginner Designs

Intermediate Designs

Advanced Designs

Appendix

The Rainbow Loom Story

Late in the summer of 2010, Cheong-Choon Ng was inspired to make the first prototype of a loom that would allow users to weave colored rubber bands into intricate patterns. Three years and 28 iterations later, this idea known as the Rainbow Loom is one of the fastest growing craft items in the nation.

The inspiration came from watching his daughters, Teresa, then aged 12, and Michelle, then aged 9, loop pony tail bands into bracelets in their Michigan home. This reminded Choon of a childhood activity of making jump ropes out of rubber bands in Malaysia. He joined them, thinking he could show his daughters how to do this, but he discovered that his fingers were now too big. This inspired him to craft a jig using wood and push pins.

His wife, Fen Chan, was not immediately impressed with his new invention. It took some time to convince his family that he was on to something big. They asked, "Why use a piece of wood when your fingers work just fine?" The reason became obvious after he showed them what he could make by looping a few geometric designs made up of rubber bands. It was his daughter Teresa that said, "Dad, kids will buy this."

In 2011, Choon filed for a patent for the Brunnian link making device and kit in honor of Hermann Brunn, the 19th century mathematician known for his work with convex geometry. The first model of the loom arrived in June of 2011 and was named Twistz Bandz. Soon after, Choon attempted to sell his loom to many stores and faced rejection over and over, but he did not let that stop him from trying. He persisted. He figured out that people did not understand what the loom could do. To solve this problem, Choon and his family created YouTube videos to demonstrate the product to others.

In 2012, Choon changed the name of his product to Rainbow Loom, after discovering a conflict with the name Twistz Bandz, and introduced new packaging. It was his niece Angelynn that suggested the new name, because "Kids love rainbows."

In July 2013, patent 8,485,565 was granted. "We developed the Rainbow Loom honestly, with hard work, painful risk and an unwavering spirit" Choon says. "It's not just a product, but an experience that we offer our customers." New patterns and uses for the loom are still being discovered.

That is the genius of the Rainbow Loom. It inspires creativity, imagination, problem solving techniques, patience, and social interaction. It also improves fine motor skills, hand-eye coordination, visual-spatial reasoning and pattern recognition. Can a product this fun be educational too? Let's discover the possibilities!

Introduction to the Rainbow Loom

The patterns in The Loomatic's Guide to the Rainbow Loom were developed and tested using the Rainbow Loom kit manufactured by Choon's Design, LLC. The Rainbow Loom kit contains 6 items: The Rainbow Loom, the hook, the mini-loom, a bag of latex-free bands, a bag of C-clips, and an Instruction Guide.

Rainbow Loom

The Rainbow Loom is made up of three clear plastic bars, containing 13 pins each. These are referred to as "bar pins". There are three removable turquoise colored base plates. The Rainbow Loom arrives in the more common "Offset" configuration but the loom can be reconfigured to a "Rectangle" configuration to allow for many more design options. See "Loom Configurations" on page 182 for more information.

Rainbow Loom Hook

The hook is a unique design with each end having a different function. The hook end is used to loop rubber bands that have been placed on the loom. The other end serves as a tool used for base plate removal. To change from one loom configuration to another, use the base plate removal tool to pry the turquoise base plates from the loom. Reassemble the loom bar pins onto the base plates and push firmly into place.

Mini Rainbow Loom

The turquoise colored mini-loom is also used as a protective cover for your hook. Storing the mini-loom over the tip of your hook offers extra protection for your hook, especially when you are on the go.

Bands

A 600 ct. bag of mixed color, synthetic rubber bands are provided in the kit. These bands are latex-free. Rainbow Loom brand refill packs are available in synthetic rubber bands and silicone bands.

C-clips

The C-clips are exclusive to Rainbow Loom. They are not sold separately but each package of Rainbow Loom refill packs contains a bag of C-clips.

How to Use The Loomatic's Guide

How To Use the QR Codes

OK, I know you're dying to try them out, so here's your first one! There are two ways to use these QR codes. First, if you have a smart phone or tablet, you can run an app that will read them. If you don't already have the app on your device, you will have to go to the App Store for your Apple device or the Play Store for Android devices. Search for "QR Code" and you will have many choices available.

startingout

Once you have the app downloaded and running, just scan the QR code and follow the directions from your app. You will be taken to YouTube where you will watch a video.

If you don't have a smart phone or tablet, you can still watch the videos on a computer. Just type into your browser: "www.loomaticsguide.com/" followed by the word under the QR code. In this example, you would type www.loomaticsguide.com/startingout. The QR Code above has "startingout" written under it. (notice where the arrow is pointing) Not all smart phones a tablets will be able to read the QR codes because of camera quality, so you may have to type the address into a browser window on your tablet or phone if it cannot read the code.

You will find QR codes throughout this book. At the beginning of each design is a QR code that will take you to a video showing you from start to finish how to make that particular bracelet or design. If you find a QR code somewhere within the instructions, it will lead you to a short video clip showing you how to complete that particular part of the instruction.

The QR code above, "startingout" covers this section of the book.

How To Use the Design Instructions

There are typically 4 parts to making a bracelet:

1) Choosing and counting out your bands.
2) Placing bands on the loom.
3) Looping the bands.
4) Finishing the bracelet.

Choosing and Counting Out Your Bands

choosing

When you find the bracelet you want to make, the first step is to fold out the back cover so you can see the page with big letters "A" through "F" on it. This is called the "Band Organizer". This is where you will put the bands to make your bracelet. A diagram of the "Band Organizer" is shown on the next page.

The Color Code Squares & Choosing Your Colors

• The Color Code Squares are located on the top left hand side of the first page of the design.

• Each Color Code Square has a letter and a number associated with it.

    Example: A & 8

• Place one rubber band of your color choice in each square.

    Example: A = Red

• The number shown in each square is the number of bands you will need.

    Example: 8 red bands are needed.

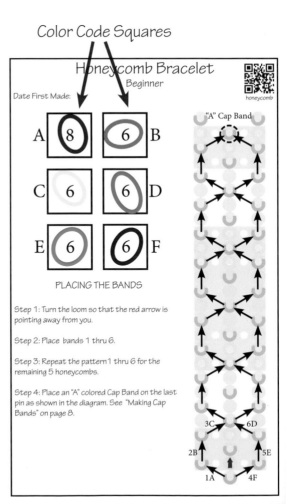

Color Code Squares

Honeycomb Bracelet
Beginner

Date First Made:

honeycomb

A 8   6 B

C 6   6 D

E 6   6 F

"A" Cap Band

PLACING THE BANDS

Step 1: Turn the loom so that the red arrow is pointing away from you.

Step 2: Place bands 1 thru 6.

Step 3: Repeat the pattern 1 thru 6 for the remaining 5 honeycombs.

Step 4: Place an "A" colored Cap Band on the last pin as shown in the diagram. See "Making Cap Bands" on page 8.

3C   6D

2B   5E

1A   4F

The Band Organizer & Counting Out Your Bands

- Make sure you have enough of each color.

  Example: 8 red bands are needed.

- Count out your bands and place them on the Band Organizer.

  Example: Count out 8 red bands and place them in the "A" section of the Band Organizer.

- Use the color code squares at the bottom of the Band Organizer if you ever need to turn your page while making a design. This will help you remember the color of band that you need to loop.

- Once you have counted out your bands you are ready to start placing them on the loom.

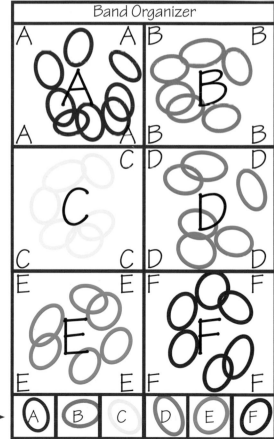

Color Code Squares →

Placing Bands on the Loom

Using your Rainbow Loom is very similar to crocheting. The most obvious reason is that a hook is used to do both things. The less obvious reason is that, in each craft, materials are linked together and connected by a looping process.

placing

When placing bands on the loom it is necessary that the instruction sheets are followed very carefully. The bands must be placed in the exact order as shown on the diagrams in order for the bands to connect correctly. Please take the time to read each step on the instruction sheets. This will save you the frustration of pulling a bracelet from the loom and watching it fall apart.

The following example will guide you through the instructions for the Honeycomb Bracelet, as shown below, and explain what each step means.

PLACING THE BANDS

To place a band, hold it between your thumb and pointer finger and stretch it from one pin to the next.

Place your bands carefully. Do not let them overlap as you place them on the pin. Keeping the bands in the right order is very important.

As you place bands, push them down onto the pin to make room for more bands to be placed above them.

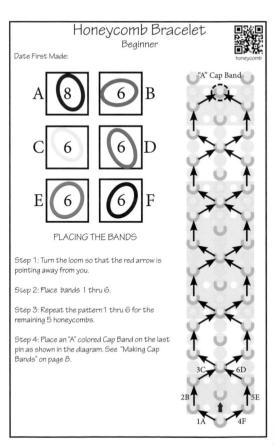

Honeycomb Bracelet
Beginner

Date First Made:

honeycomb

"A" Cap Band

A	8	6	B
C	6	6	D
E	6	6	F

PLACING THE BANDS

Step 1: Turn the loom so that the red arrow is pointing away from you.

Step 2: Place bands 1 thru 6.

Step 3: Repeat the pattern 1 thru 6 for the remaining 5 honeycombs.

Step 4: Place an "A" colored Cap Band on the last pin as shown in the diagram. See "Making Cap Bands" on page 8.

3C   6D

2B   5E

1A   4F

Step 1: Turn the loom so that the red arrow is pointing away from you.

- When the red arrow is pointed away from you, the curved sides of the pins are facing you. You will use the curved side of the pins to pull your bands against as you place them.

Step 2: Place bands 1 thru 6.

- Each band is shown as an arrow in the diagram. Each arrow has a number and letter associated with it. The number tells you the order the band is placed, the letter tells you the color of the band to use. .

  Example: Look for the arrow marked 1A. The number 1 means that this is the first band placed and the letter "A" tells you the color of band to use. See the Color Code Squares to determine the color.

- The placement of the arrow shows where to put the band. The order that the bands are placed on the loom is very important. Say the number of each band as you place it on the loom so you keep them in order

  Example: Band 1A is stretched between the first middle pin and the first pin on the left side of the loom.

Step 3: Repeat the pattern 1 thru 6 for the remaining 5 honeycombs.

- This means that you repeat the same pattern you just completed starting from where the last pattern ended.

- To minimize confusion, the duplicate patterns will not be labeled on the loom. Look at the original pattern and repeat it.

Step 4: Place an "A" colored Cap Band on the last pin.

- The Cap Band is shown at the top of the diagram as a dashed circle. The next section will show you how to make a Cap Band.

Making Cap Bands

A "Cap Band" is a band that is double looped. The Cap Band is the last band that is placed on many bracelet designs, creating a finished appearance when it is removed from the loom.

A Cap Band is shown in this book as a dashed circle around a pin. In the example shown in the diagram to the right, you are to place an "A" colored Cap Band on the pin shown.

"A" Cap Band

To make a Cap Band, put two fingers from each hand through the center of the band.

Stretch the band and twist it into a "figure 8"

and then loop the band back upon itself. This forms a double looped band, or what I call a Cap Band.

The Cap Band is then placed over the pin. Notice how the blue Cap Band wraps around the pin two times.

Looping The Bands

After placing the bands on the loom, the next step is to loop them. When looping bands, you are doing just that; looping one band through one or more other bands. It is during this process that most mistakes are made. You must follow the looping instructions very carefully. If you miss any one band, your entire bracelet will fall apart.

looping

How to Hold Your Hook

You will use your hook to loop the bands. Hold the hook like you would a pencil; only hold the hook more upright. The open side of the hook must be facing away from you.

Now, let's continue with the Honeycomb Bracelet example.

Step 5: Turn the loom around so that the red arrow is pointing toward you.

When the red arrow is toward you, the open sides of the pins, or the channels, are facing you.

Step 6: Loop bands 1 thru 6.

- Each band to be looped is shown as an arrow in the diagram. The direction the arrow points indicates the direction the band is to be looped. The direction a band is looped is very important.

- The looping order of the bands is shown as a number. The letter following the number indicates the color of the band you will be looping.

Example: Look for the arrow marked 1D. The number 1 means

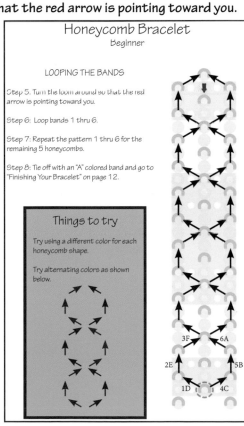

Honeycomb Bracelet
Beginner

LOOPING THE BANDS

Step 5. Turn the loom around so that the red arrow is pointing toward you.

Step 6: Loop bands 1 thru 6.

Step 7: Repeat the pattern 1 thru 6 for the remaining 5 honeycombs.

Step 8: Tie off with an "A" colored band and go to "Finishing Your Bracelet" on page 12.

Things to try

Try using a different color for each honeycomb shape.

Try alternating colors as shown below.

3F   6A
2E   5B
1D   4C

that this is the first band looped and from the Color Code Square, the letter "D" lets you know it's a green band.

- When looping, you slide the hook down the channel of the pin until you get to the band you need to loop. In the case of 1D, you will be sliding your hook inside of the red Cap Band and grabbing the green band that is just below it. You will need to hold the Cap Band with your finger to keep it from coming off from the pin.

Step 7: Repeat the pattern 1 thru 6 for the remaining 5 honeycombs.

- This means that you repeat the same pattern you just completed starting from where the last pattern ended.

- Every band must be looped in the numerical order shown.

Step 8: Tie off with an "A" colored band and go to "Finishing Your Bracelet" on page 12.

- This step is explained in the section "Finishing Your Bracelet" on page 12.

The Loomatics Tips and Tricks

tricks

Placing the Bands
- Place your bands carefully. Do not let them overlap as you place them on the pin. Keeping the bands in the right order is very important.
- Try not to twist your bands as you place them on the loom. Hold the band between your thumb and pointer finger and stretch it from one pin and past the other. Let it snap into place on the pin.
- Do not use stretched out rubber bands. Save these for practice!
- Check the rubber bands as you are placing them for weak spots and thin areas.

Looping
- Check for any twisted bands before you start looping. If you see any bands that are twisted, a quick way to untwist them is to run your hook around the outside of the pin, between the pin and the bands. Circle the pin a few times with your hook and this will straighten out your bands. For a demo, watch the "tricks" video by scanning the QR code above.
- Think of this phrase as you are looping, "Stay LOW as you go!" If you pull your hook up too high while you are looping the bands will pop off the pins. If you stay low, the bands will stay on!
- Think of this phrase as you are looping, "Up and over and ALL the way around!" As you are looping, you will need to gently ease the band up and over the lip of the first pin, and then move your hook ALL the way around the pin you are looping to.
- Look for the pull or tightening of the band as you pull a band. This will show you that you are looping the right band.
- As you loop the bands notice that they will usually form a "tear drop" shape when they are looped back correctly upon themselves.

Using Your Hook
- Protect your tip! Never use the tip of your hook to pull a bracelet off from the loom. The tip may break. Instead, pull the bands to the thickest part of the hook before you pull the bracelet off.
- Keep the open side of the hook pointing in the direction that you are looping. If the open side of the hook is turned toward you while you are looping, the band will slide off.
- If a band slides up on your hook, tilt your hook upright to move the band back into the correct position.
- Tilt your hook forward to release the band when you have completed looping.

Finishing Your Bracelet

finishing

If you are just beginning to make bracelets, I highly suggest you watch the video on finishing a bracelet. This procedure will be done after each and every bracelet in the book.

Tying off your bracelet is covered in steps 1 thru 4.

Step 1: Turn the loom so the red arrow is pointing away from you.

Step 2: On the last pin looped (the one closest to you now), push all of the bands to the top of the pin as shown in the photo.

Step 3: Slide the hook down through the channel of the pin, through all of the bands, and tilt it to the side. Put a rubber band on the hook as shown.

Step 4: Holding onto one end of the band, pull the other end of the band back up through the channel of the pin. Put the hook through both ends of the band and slide the band up to the thickest part of the hook as shown in the photo.

Step 5: Remove the bracelet from the loom. To do this, use your fingers to pull the looped bands up over the lip of the last pin. Continue to pull the bracelet off of the loom by pulling up and back. Leave the bracelet on the hook and set it aside.

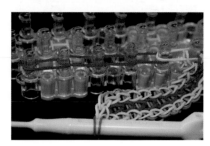

Step 6: Extend the braclet. To do this, make a single chain of bands up one side of the loom. These bands are red in the photo. The last band you place in the single chain is the cap band on the end of the bracelet. The cap band in the photo is yellow.

For most children, 3 or 4 bands in the single chain should work. For most adults, 6 or 7 bands will be required.

Step 7: Without removing the bracelet from the hook, loop the single chain. Place a C-clip over the last band looped, remove from the loom and connect the two ends of the bracelet with the C-clip.

Tips

Beginner level users may want to slip knot a rubber band around the loose end of the bracelet until they feel confident attaching a C-clip. To make a slip knot, slide a rubber band through the loose ends of a bracelet and fold in half. Push one end of the folded band through the opening created by the other. Grab it and pull it tight to secure the ends of the bracelet.

It is extremely important that all bands are captured by the C-clip when it is applied. Look closely at the C-clip. One half of the bands should be pulled to one side of the C-clip and the other half should be pulled to the other side.

Things to try

When extending your bracelet, try alternating the colors of bands.

When extending an advanced or thicker bracelet, try using two bands at a time.

Beginner Designs

Single Chain Bracelet
Beginner

Date First Made:

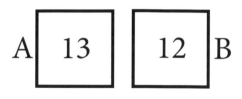

| A | 13 | 12 | B |

PLACING THE BANDS

Step 1: Turn the loom so that the red arrow is pointing away from you.

Step 2: Following the diagram to the right, place bands 1 and 2. Note you will be alternating colors between A & B as you move up the loom.

Step 3: Repeat this 1 - 2 pattern to the end of the loom.

Things to try

Try making a ring by using 6 to 8 bands and connect with a C-clip.

Make a Fuzzy Bracelet! Before pulling the bracelet off from the loom, slip knot or tie 2 bands to each loop. Carefully snip the ends with scissors. Be careful not to cut your bracelet!

Fuzzy Bracelet design submitted by Lori LaRosa, Marlton, N.J.

Single Chain Bracelet
Beginner

LOOPING THE BANDS

Step 4: Turn the loom around so that the red arrow is pointing toward you.

Step 5: Loop bands 1 and 2 as shown in the diagram.

Step 6: Repeat the 1 - 2 pattern to the end of the loom.

Be sure to loop the bands in the order shown in the diagram or your bracelet will fall apart.

Step 7: Place a C-clip over the last band that you looped.

Step 8: Remove the bracelet from the loom and attach the two ends with the C-clip.

Note: This arrow is greyed out because you will not be looping it. You will start looping at the second band labeled "1B", meaning it's the first band you'll loop, and it's a "B" colored band.

Note: You can adjust the length of the bracelet by moving the C-clip to a different link on the chain.

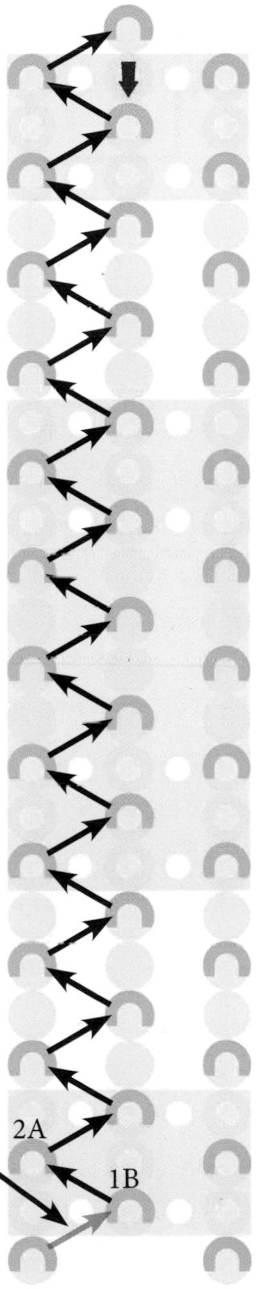

2A

1B

Diamond Bracelet
Beginner

diamond

Date First Made:

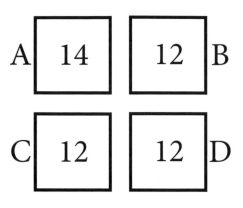

| A | 14 | 12 | B |
| C | 12 | 12 | D |

PLACING THE BANDS

Step 1: Place the loom so that the red arrow is pointing away from you.

Step 2: Following the diagram to the right, place bands 1 thru 4.

Step 3: Repeat the pattern 1 thru 4 to the end of the loom.

Step 4: Place an "A" colored Cap Band on the last pin as shown in the diagram. See "Making Cap Bands" on page 8.

Hint: As you place each band, push it down on the pin to make room for more bands to be placed above.

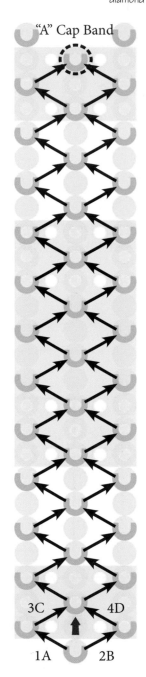

"A" Cap Band

3C   4D

1A   2B

Diamond Bracelet
Beginner

LOOPING THE BANDS

Step 5: Turn the loom around so that the red arrow is pointing toward you.

Step 6: Using the diagram to the right, loop the bands 1 thru 4.

Step 7: Repeat the pattern 1 thru 4 to the end of the loom.

Step 8: Tie off with an "A" colored band and go to "Finishing Your Bracelet" on page 12.

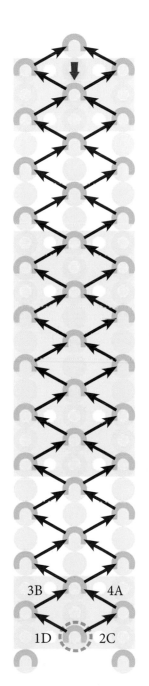

3B   4A

1D   2C

Things to try

Try using a different color for each diamond shape.

Place two bands at a time to make an extra thick bracelet.

Diamond Ridge Bracelet
Beginner

Date First Made:

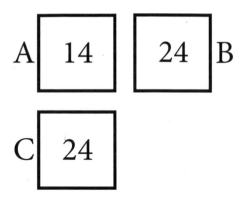

A | 14   24 | B

C | 24

PLACING THE BANDS

Step 1: Turn the loom so that the red arrow is pointing away from you.

Step 2: Place bands 1 thru 12.

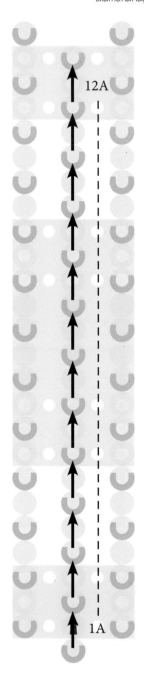

Diamond Ridge Bracelet
Beginner

PLACING THE BANDS

Step 3: Place bands 1 thru 8.

Step 4: Repeat the pattern 1 thru 8 to the end of the loom.

Step 5: Place an "A" colored Cap Band on the last pin as shown in the diagram. See "Making Cap Bands" on page 8.

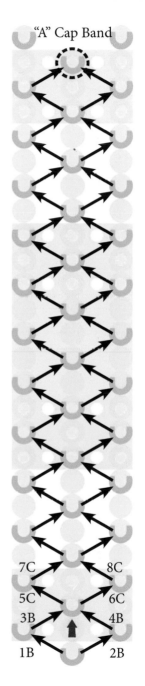

"A" Cap Band

7C   8C
5C   6C
3B   4B
1B   2B

Diamond Ridge Bracelet
Beginner

Date First Made:

LOOPING THE BANDS

Step 6: Turn the loom around so that the red arrow is pointing toward you.

Step 7: Loop bands 1 thru 10.

Step 8: Repeat the pattern 1 thru 10 to the end of the loom.

Step 9: Tie off with an "A" colored band and go to "Finishing Your Bracelet" on page 12.

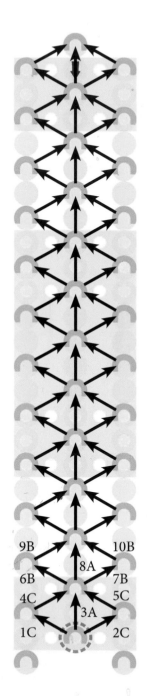

Honeycomb Bracelet
Beginner

Date First Made:

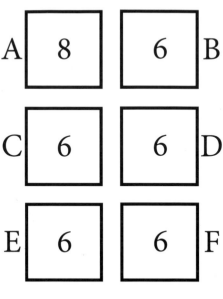

A **8**	**6** B
C **6**	**6** D
E **6**	**6** F

PLACING THE BANDS

Step 1: Turn the loom so that the red arrow is pointing away from you.

Step 2: Place bands 1 thru 6.

Step 3: Repeat the pattern 1 thru 6 for the remaining 5 honeycombs.

Step 4: Place an "A" colored Cap Band on the last pin as shown in the diagram. See "Making Cap Bands" on page 8.

Tip
The order in which the bands are placed and looped is very important. Say the number of the band out loud as you place it or loop it.

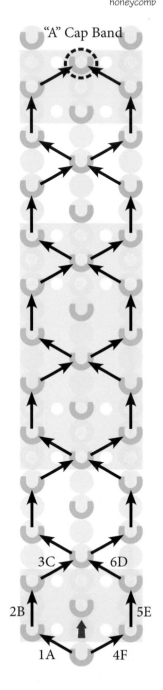

"A" Cap Band

3C   6D

2B   5E

1A   4F

Honeycomb Bracelet
Beginner

LOOPING THE BANDS

Step 5: Turn the loom around so that the red arrow is pointing toward you.

Step 6: Loop bands 1 thru 6.

Step 7: Repeat the pattern 1 thru 6 for the remaining 5 honeycombs.

Step 8: Tie off with an "A" colored band and go to "Finishing Your Bracelet" on page 12.

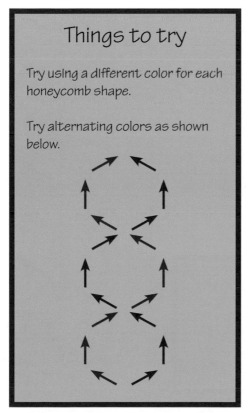

Things to try

Try using a different color for each honeycomb shape.

Try alternating colors as shown below.

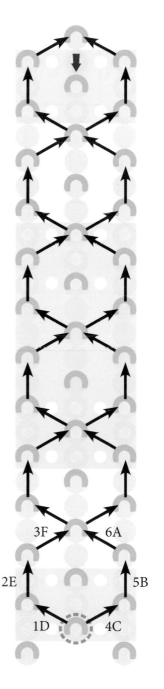

3F   6A

2E   5B

1D   4C

Single Rhombus Bracelet
Beginner

srhombus

Date First Made:

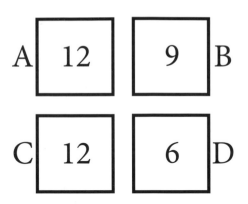

| A | 12 | 9 | B |
| C | 12 | 6 | D |

PLACING THE BANDS

Step 1: Place the loom so that the red arrow is pointing away from you.

Step 2: Place bands 1 thru 6.

Step 3: Repeat the pattern 1 thru 6 to the end of the loom. Make sure you place the last band labeled "1B".

Step 4: Place a "B" colored Cap Band on the last pin as shown in the diagram. See "Making Cap Bands" on page 8.

Things To Try

Make the "Caterpillar Bracelet":
A (Black)   B (Red)
C (Pink)   D (Green)

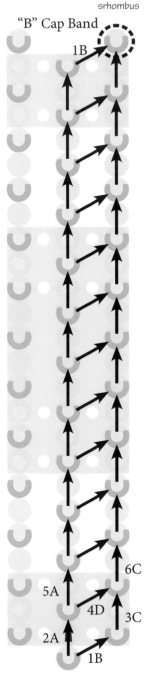

"B" Cap Band

1B

6C
5A
4D
3C
2A
1B

Single Rhombus Bracelet
Beginner

LOOPING THE BANDS

Step 5: Turn the loom around so that the red arrow is pointing toward you.

Step 6: Loop bands 1 thru 6.

Step 7: Repeat the pattern 1 thru 6 to the end of the loom. Make sure you loop the last band labeled "1B".

Step 8: Tie off with a "B" colored band and go to "Finishing Your Bracelet" on page 12.

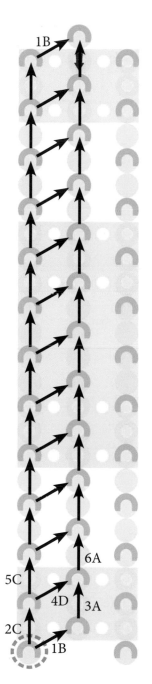

Triangle Bracelet
Beginner

Date First Made:

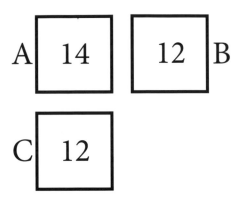

A [14]   [12] B

C [12]

PLACING THE BANDS

Step 1: Turn the loom so that the red arrow is pointing away from you.

Step 2: Place bands 1 thru 6.

Step 3: Repeat the pattern 1 thru 6 to the end of the loom.

Step 4: Place an "A" colored Cap Band on the last pin as shown in the diagram. See "Making Cap Bands" on page 8.

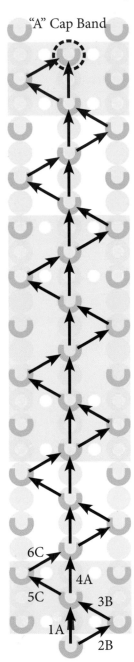

"A" Cap Band

6C
5C
4A
3B
1A
2B

Triangle Bracelet
Beginner

LOOPING THE BANDS

Step 5: Turn the loom so that the red arrow is pointing toward you.

Step 6: Loop bands 1 thru 6.

Step 7: Repeat the pattern 1 thru 6 to the end of the loom.

Step 8: Tie off with an "A" colored band and go to "Finishing Your Bracelet" on page 12.

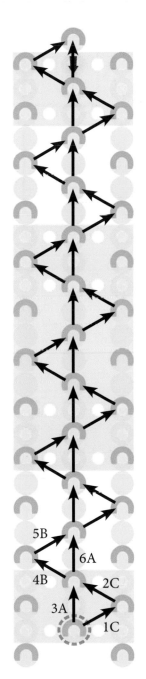

Speckled Rhombus Bracelet
Beginner

Date First Made:

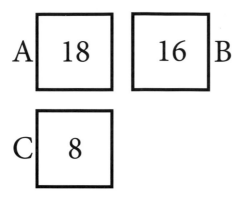

A [18]   [16] B

C [8]

PLACING THE BANDS

Step 1: Place the loom so that the red arrow is pointing away from you.

Step 2: Place bands 1 thru 10. Make sure you pay attention to the color of each band.

Step 3: Repeat the pattern 1 thru 10 to the end of the loom.

Step 4: Place an "A" colored Cap Band on the last pin as shown in the diagram. See "Making Cap Bands" on page 8.

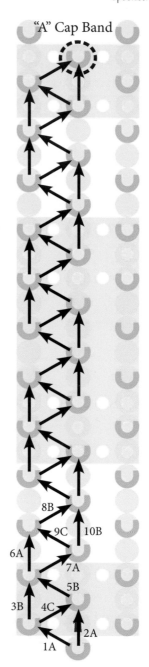

"A" Cap Band

8B
9C   10B
6A
7A
5B
3B   4C
1A   2A

Speckled Rhombus Bracelet
Beginner

LOOPING THE BANDS

Step 5: Turn the loom around so that the red arrow is pointing toward you.

Step 6: Loop bands 1 thru 10.

Step 7: Repeat the pattern 1 thru 10 to the end of the loom.

Step 8: Tie off with an "A" colored band and go to "Finishing Your Bracelet" on page 12.

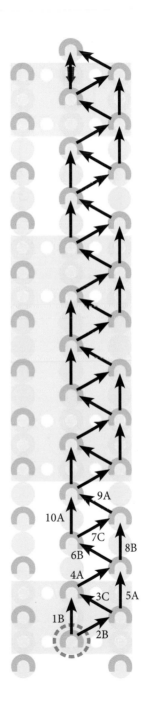

Diamond Trio Bracelet
Beginner

diamondtrio

Date First Made:

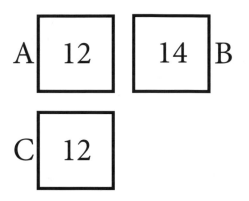

"B" Cap Band

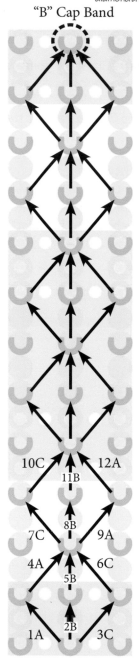

PLACING THE BANDS

Step 1: Convert the loom from an "offset" to a "rectangle" configuration. To learn how to do this, see "Loom Configurations" on page 182.

Step 2: Turn the loom so that the red arrow is pointing away from you.

Step 3: Place bands 1 thru 12.

Step 4: Repeat the pattern 1 thru 12 two more times.

Step 5: Place a "B" colored Cap Band on the last pin as shown in the diagram. See "Making Cap Bands" on page 8.

Diamond Trio Bracelet
Beginner

LOOPING THE BANDS

Step 6: Turn the loom around so that the red arrow is pointing toward you.

Step 7: Loop bands 1 thru 12.

Step 8: Repeat the pattern 1 thru 12 to the end of the loom.

Step 9: Tie off with a "B" colored band and go to "Finishing Your Bracelet" on page 12.

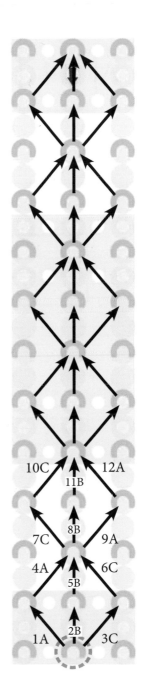

Spiral Bracelet
Beginner

Date First Made:

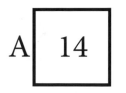 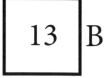

A | 14 | 13 | B

PLACING THE BANDS

"A" Cap Band

Step 1: Turn the loom so that the red arrow is pointing away from you.

Step 2: Place band 1 as shown below.

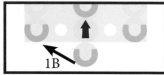

Step 3: Place bands 1 thru 4 as shown in the diagram to the right and also in the diagram below. To make this design a little easier, the "A" bands have been highlighted in blue. Notice how each zig-zag pattern is a different color. Blue touches blue, black touches black.

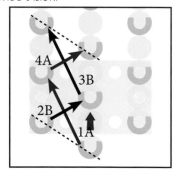

Step 4: Repeat the pattern 1 thru 4 five more times.

Step 5: Place an "A" colored Cap Band on the last pin as shown in the diagram. See "Making Cap Bands" on page 8.

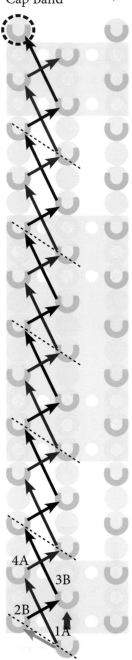

Spiral Bracelet
Beginner

LOOPING THE BANDS

Step 6: Turn the loom around so that the red arrow is pointing toward you.

Step 7: Loop bands 1 thru 4 as shown in the diagram to the right and also below.

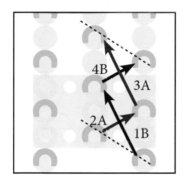

Step 8: Repeat the pattern 1 thru 4 to the end of the loom.

Step 9: Loop band 1 as shown at the top of the diagram.

Step 10: Tie off with an "A" colored band and go to "Finishing Your Bracelet" on page 12.

Things to try

Try 2 bands at a time to make an extra thick Sprial Bracelet.

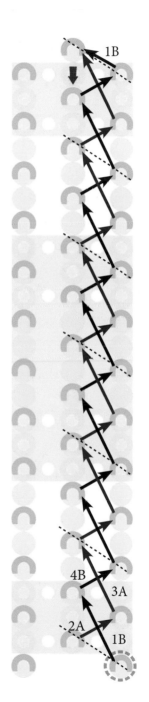

Bead Ladder Bracelet
Beginner

Date First Made:

A 28 10 B

PLACING THE BANDS

Step 1: Turn the loom so that the red arrow is pointing away from you.

Step 2: Thread 10 bands through 10 pony beads. These will be your "B" bands.

Step 3: Place bands 1 thru 13.

Step 4: Place bands 14 thru 26 .

Step 5: Place bands 27 thru 36 using the "B" bead bands you made in Step 2.

Step 6: Place an "A" colored Cap Band on the last pin as shown in the diagram. See "Making Cap Bands" on page 8.

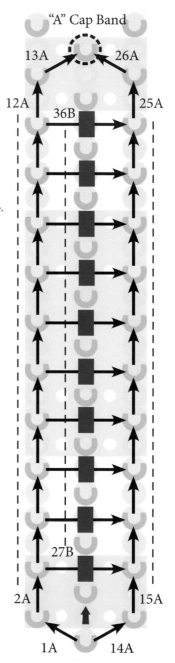

Bead Ladder Bracelet
Beginner

LOOPING THE BANDS

Step 7: Turn the loom around so that the red arrow is pointing toward you.

Step 8: Loop bands 1 thru 13.

Step 9: Loop bands 14 thru 26.

Step 10: Tie off with an "A" colored band and go to "Finishing Your Bracelet" on page 12.

Tips

6 mm to 9mm pony beads work best. Try using other beads or decorative buttons.

A 3.5mm crochet hook may be useful to help pull the bands through the pony beads.

You can also use an orthodonic floss threader to pull the bands through the beads.

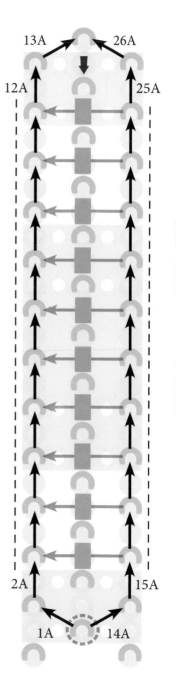

Triple Single Bracelet
Beginner

triplesingle

Date First Made:

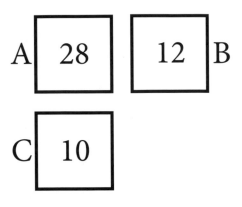

A | 28

12 | B

C | 10

PLACING THE BANDS

Step 1: Place the loom so that the red arrow is pointing away from you.

Step 2: Place bands 1 thru 13.

Step 3: Place bands 14 thru 26.

Step 4: Place bands 27 thru 38.

Step 5: Place an "A" colored Cap Band on the last pin as shown in the diagram. See "Making Cap Bands" on page 8.

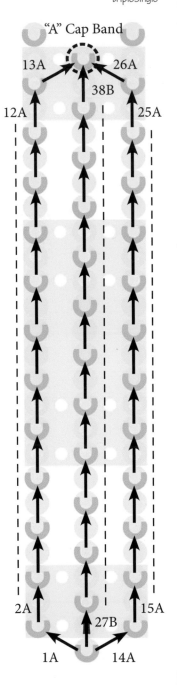

"A" Cap Band

13A   26A

38B

12A   25A

2A   15A

27B

1A   14A

Triple Single Bracelet
Beginner

PLACING THE BANDS

Step 6: Push all of the bands down on the pins making room for more bands on top.

Step 7: Place bands 1 thru 10. Notice these bands stretch around three pins forming a triangle shape. Be sure you skip the first and last row of pins as shown in the diagram.

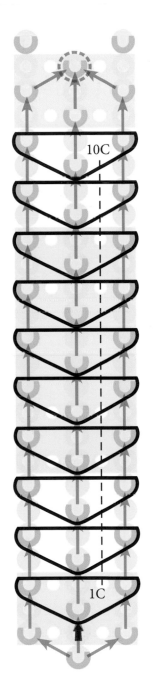

Things to try

Try alternating colors.

Place two bands at a time to make an extra thick bracelet. (Don't use two bands for the triangles.)

Stagger or make different shapes while placing the bands when placing the "A" and "B" bands.

Connect two looms, end-to-end, to make a full length bracelet.

Triple Single Bracelet
Beginner

LOOPING THE BANDS

Step 8: Turn the loom around so that the red arrow is pointing toward you.

Step 9: Loop bands 1 thru 12.

Step 10: Loop bands 13 thru 25.

Step 11: Loop bands 26 thru 38.

Step 12: Tie off with an "A" colored band and go to "Finishing Your Bracelet" on page 12.

Note: When looping the sides of the loom, you must make sure you loop through the "C" triangle bands. To do this, use the back of your hook to pull the "C" bands back before grabbing the two bottom bands. See the photos on the next page.

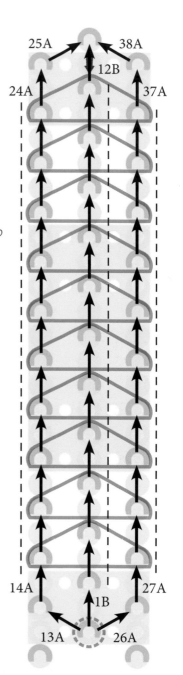

Looping the Triple Single

ts_looping

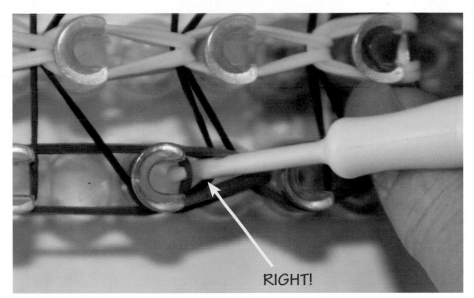

RIGHT!

CORRECT: When looping the bands along the sides of the loom, you must use the back of the hook to pull the black "C" bands back while grabbing the bottom red "A" band. Notice how the red band is being pulled through the black band.

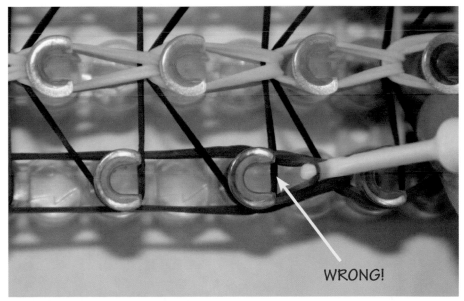

WRONG!

INCORRECT: Notice how the red band is not being pulled through the black triangle band, it is being pulled behind it. If you do this, your bracelet will fall apart as you pull it off the loom.

Triple Single Backpack Tag
Beginner

Date First Made:

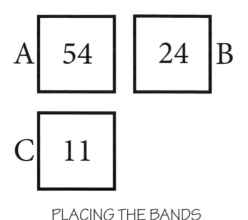

A | 54

24 | B

C | 11

PLACING THE BANDS

Step 1: Place the loom so that the red arrow is pointing away from you.

Step 2: Place bands 1 thru 13 using two bands at a time. See the note below.

Step 3: Place bands 14 thru 26 using two bands at a time.

Step 4: Place bands 27 thru 38 using two bands at a time.

Note: You will be placing two bands at a time, one on top the other. Place them one at a time to avoid twisting the bands.

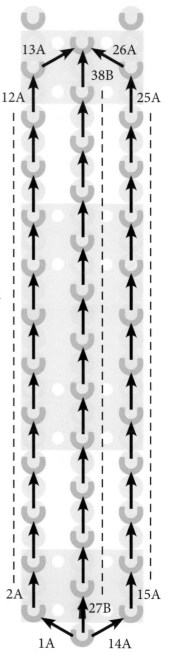

Triple Single Backpack Tag
Beginner

PLACING THE BANDS

Step 5: Push all of the bands down on the pins making room for more bands on top.

Step 6: Using only one "C" colored band at a time, place bands 1 thru 11. These bands will be stretched around three pins to form a triangle shape. Be sure you skip the first and last row of pins as shown in the diagram.

11C

Make certain that the first triangle is placed here and not at the bottom of the loom.

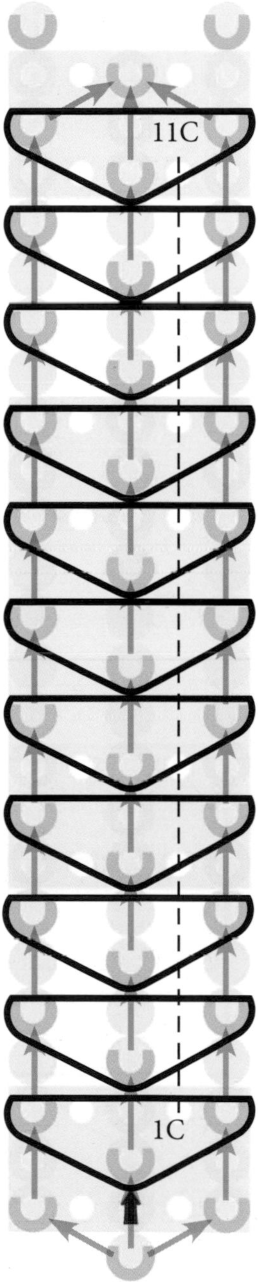

1C

Triple Single Backpack Tag
Beginner

LOOPING THE BANDS

Step 7: Turn the loom around so that the red arrow is pointing toward you.

Step 8: Place the key ring over the bottom middle pin. See the diagram to the right.

Step 9: Loop bands 1 thru 12. **Make sure you grab two bands at a time when looping!** See the note below.

Step 10: Loop bands 13 thru 25.

Step 11: Loop bands 26 thru 38.

Step 12: Tie off with two "A" colored bands (instead of the usual one) and add a C-clip to finish.

Note: When looping the sides of the loom, you must make sure you loop through the "C" triangle bands. To do this, use the back of your hook to pull the "C" bands back before grabbing the two bottom bands. See the photos on the next page.

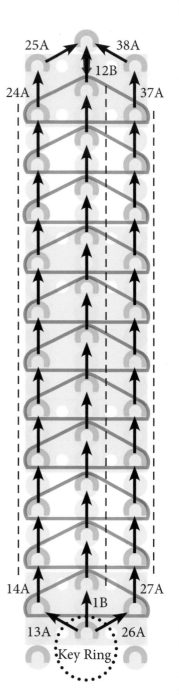

Looping the
Triple Single

ts_looping

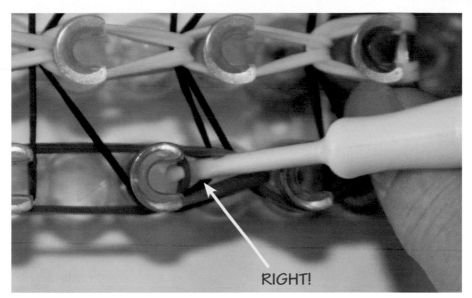

RIGHT!

CORRECT: When looping the bands along the sides of the loom, you must use the back of the hook to pull the black "C" bands back while grabbing the two bottom red "A" bands. Notice how the red bands are being pulled through the black band.

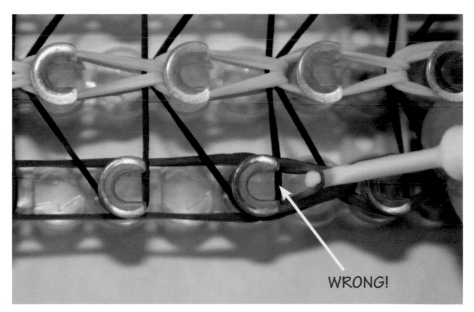

WRONG!

INCORRECT: Notice how the red bands are not being pulled through the black triangle band. If you do this, your backpack tag will fall apart as you pull it off the loom.

Intermediate Designs

Taffy Twist Bracelet
Intermediate
Submitted by Ally Aufman
Wexford, PA

x

Taffy Twist Bracelet
Intermediate

PLACING THE BANDS

Step 5: Place bands 1 thru 12 using three bands at a time (A, B, and C). Twist them to form a figure eight and stretch across the outer pins as shown in the diagram to the right and in the photo below.

Each band shown here is actually 3 bands (A, B, & C) twisted together to form a figure eight.

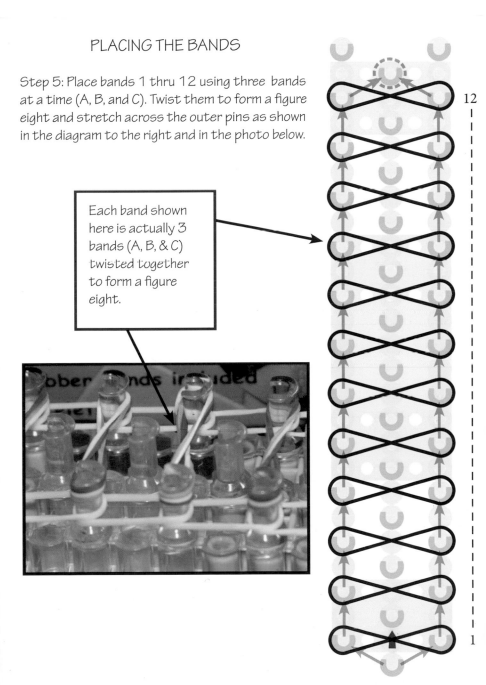

Taffy Twist Bracelet
Intermediate

LOOPING THE BANDS

Step 6: Turn the loom around so that the red arrow is pointing toward you.

Step 7: Loop bands 1 thru 13.

Step 8: Loop bands 14 thru 26.

Step 9: Tie off with an "A" colored band and go to "Finishing Your Bracelet" on page 12.

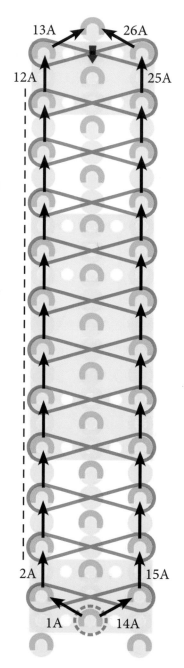

Double Bead Ladder Bracelet

Intermediate

doublebead

Date First Made:

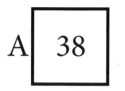

A **38** **12** B

PLACING THE BANDS

Step 1: Place 2 pony beads over 10 of the "A" colored bands. Set them aside until Step 7.

Step 2: Turn the loom so that the red arrow is pointing away from you.

Step 3: Place bands 1 thru 13.

Step 4: Place bands 14 thru 26.

Step 5: Place bands 27 thru 38.

Step 6: Place an "A" colored Cap Band on the last pin as shown in the diagram. See "Making Cap Bands" on page 8.

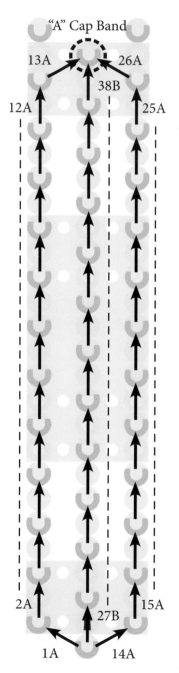

Double Bead Ladder Bracelet
Intermediate

PLACING THE BANDS

Step 7: Place bands 1 thru 10 using the bands with 2 pony beads on them.

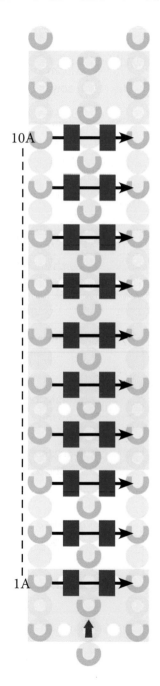

Double Bead Ladder Bracelet
Intermediate

LOOPING THE BANDS

Step 8: Turn the loom around so that the red arrow is pointing toward you.

Step 9: Loop the bead bands 1 thru 12 as shown in the diagram. You will be looping the bands between the beads as shown in the diagram.

Step 10: Loop bands 13 thru 25.

Step 11: Loop bands 26 thru 38.

Step 12: Tie off with an "A" colored band and go to "Finishing Your Bracelet" on page 12.

Tips

6 mm to 9mm pony beads work best. Other beads may also work.

A 3.5mm crochet hook may be useful to help pull the bands through the pony beads.

You can also use an orthodonic floss threader to pull the bands through the beads.

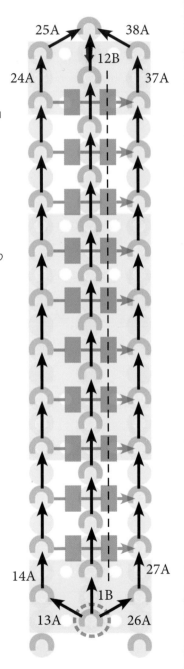

Rainbow Ladder Bracelet
Intermediate

ladder

Date First Made:

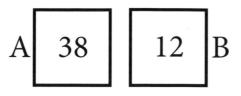

A | 38 | 12 | B

PLACING THE BANDS

Step 1: Turn the loom so that the red arrow is pointing away from you.

Step 2: Place bands 1 thru 13.

Step 3: Place bands 14 thru 26.

Step 4: Place bands 27 thru 36.

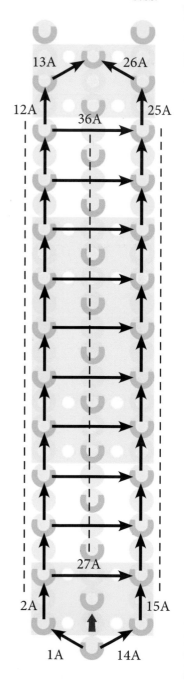

Rainbow Ladder Bracelet
Intermediate

PLACING THE BANDS

Step 5: Place bands 1 thru 12.

Step 6: Place an "A" colored Cap Band on the last pin as shown in the diagram. See "Making Cap Bands" on page 8.

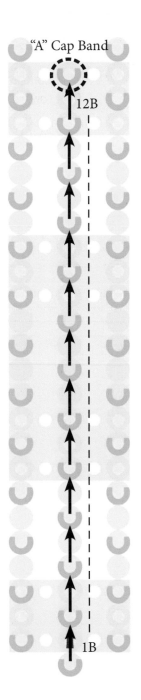

"A" Cap Band

12B

1B

Things to try

For a rainbow effect, use 2 each of red, orange, yellow, green, blue, and purple for the "B" colored bands. Place them in R-O-Y-G-B-P order and repeat R-O-Y-G-B-P to complete a rainbow stripe.

Reverse it! Place your "A" bands in rainbow order and use black bands for your "B" bands.

Rainbow Ladder Bracelet
Intermediate

LOOPING THE BANDS

Step 7: Turn the loom around so that the red arrow is pointing toward you.

Step 8: Loop bands 1 thru 12 as shown in the diagram.

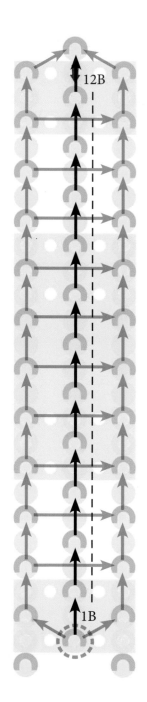

Rainbow Ladder Bracelet
Intermediate

PLACING MORE BANDS

Step 9: Place bands 1 thru 10 as shown in the diagram. These bands are placed directly above the bands placed in Step 4.

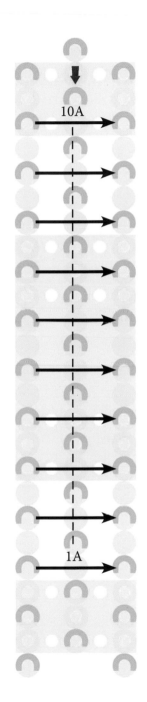

Rainbow Ladder Bracelet
Intermediate

LOOPING MORE BANDS

Step 10: Loop bands 1 thru 13.

Step 11: Loop bands 14 thru 26.

Step 12: Tie off with an "A" colored band and go to "Finishing Your Bracelet" on page 12.

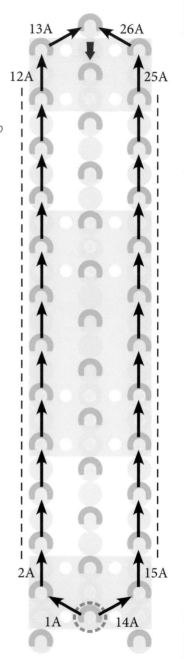

Zippy Chain Bracelet
Intermediate

Date First Made:

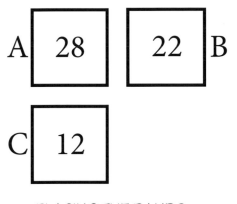

A 28   22 B

C 12

PLACING THE BANDS

Step 1: Turn the loom so that the red arrow is pointing away from you.

Step 2: Place bands 1 thru 13.

Step 3: Place bands 14 thru 26.

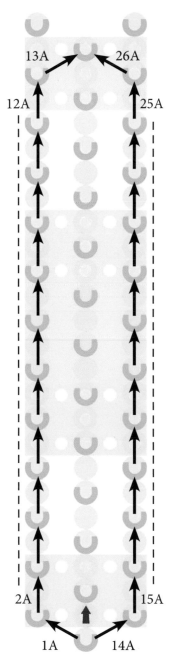

13A   26A

12A   25A

2A   15A

1A   14A

Zippy Chain Bracelet
Intermediate

PLACING THE BANDS

Step 4: Place bands 1 thru 3.

Step 5: Repeat the pattern 1 thru 3 to the end of the loom.

Step 6: Place an "A" colored Cap Band on the last pin as shown in the diagram. See "Making Cap Bands" on page 8.

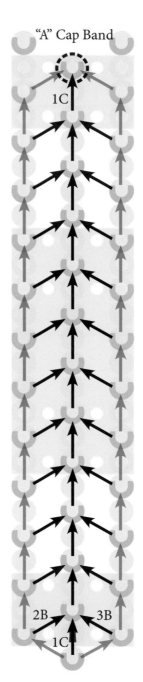

"A" Cap Band

1C

2B   3B

1C

Zippy Chain Bracelet
Intermediate

LOOPING THE BANDS

Step 7: Turn the loom around so that the red arrow is pointing toward you.

Step 8: Loop bands 1 thru 5 as shown in the diagram below.

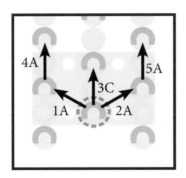

Step 9: Loop bands 1 thru 5 as shown in the diagram to the right.

Step 10: Repeat the pattern 1 thru 5 to the end of the loom. On the last row, bands 4 and 5 are looped to the center pin.

Step 11: Tie off with an "A" colored band and go to "Finishing Your Bracelet" on page 12.

Holiday Bracelet
Intermediate

Date First Made:

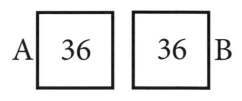

A | 36 | 36 | B

PLACING THE BANDS

Step 1: Turn the loom so that the red arrow is pointing away from you.

Step 2: Place bands 1 thru 13.

Step 3: Place bands 14 thru 26.

Step 4: Place an "A" colored Cap Band on the last pin as shown in the diagram. See "Making Cap Bands" on page 8.

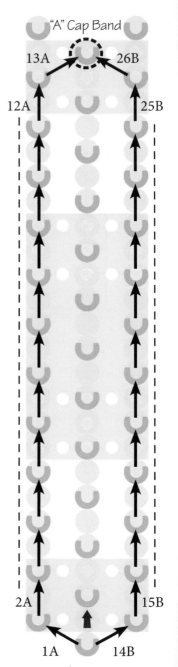

Holiday Bracelet
Intermediate

PLACING THE BANDS

Step 5: Place bands 1 thru 4. Notice the bands alternate from "A" colored to "B" colored. It is very important that you place these in the right order.

Step 6: Repeat the pattern 1 thru 4 to the end of the loom.

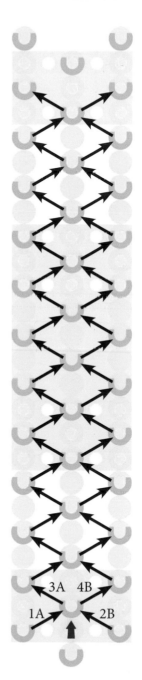

Holiday Bracelet
Intermediate

LOOPING THE BANDS

Step 7: Turn the loom around so that the red arrow is pointing toward you.

Step 8: Loop bands 1 thru 6.

Step 9: Repeat the pattern 1 thru 6 to the end of the loom.

Step 10: Tie off with a "B" colored band and go to "Finishing Your Bracelet" on page 12.

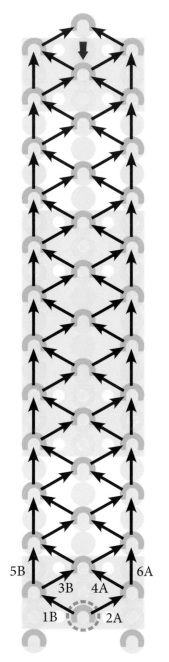

5B   6A

3B   4A

1B   2A

Liberty Twist Bracelet
Intermediate

Date First Made:

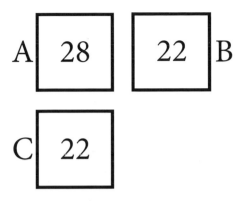

A | 28   22 | B

C | 22

PLACING THE BANDS

Step 1: Place the loom so that the red arrow is pointing away from you.

Step 2: Place bands 1 thru 13.

Step 3: Place bands 14 thru 26.

Step 4: Place an "A" colored Cap Band on the last pin as shown in the diagram. See "Making Cap Bands" on page 8.

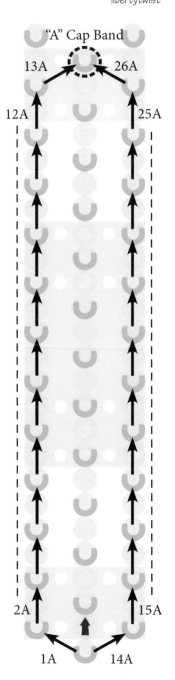

"A" Cap Band

13A   26A

12A   25A

2A   15A

1A   14A

Liberty Twist Bracelet
Intermediate

PLACING THE BANDS

Step 5: Place bands 1 thru 4.

Step 6: Repeat the pattern 1 thru 4 to the end of the loom.

Liberty Twist Bracelet
Intermediate

LOOPING THE BANDS

Step 7: Turn the loom around, so that the red arrow is pointing toward you.

Step 8: Loop bands 1 & 2 as shown in the diagram below.

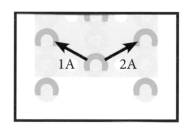

Step 9: Loop bands 1 thru 12 as shown in the diagram on the right.

Step 10: Repeat the pattern 1 thru 12 to the end of the loom. On the last group, bands 7 & 8 are looped to the center pin.

Step 11: Tie off with an "A" colored band and go to "Finishing Your Bracelet" on page 12.

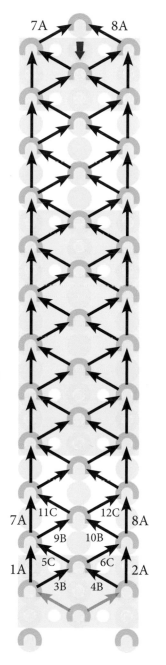

Team Spirit Bracelet
Intermediate

teamspirit

Date First Made:

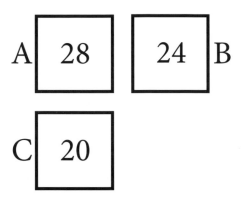

| A | 28 | 24 | B |
| C | 20 | | |

PLACING THE BANDS

Step 1: Turn the loom so that the red arrow is pointing away from you.

Step 2: Place bands 1 thru 13.

Step 3: Place bands 14 thru 26.

Step 4: Place an "A" colored Cap Band on the last pin as shown in the diagram. See "Making Cap Bands" on page 8.

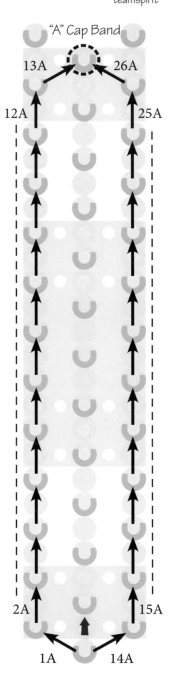

Team Spirit Bracelet
Intermediate

PLACING THE BANDS

Step 5: Place bands 1 thru 8.

Step 6: Repeat the pattern 1 thru 8 to the end of the loom. The pattern will end on 3B - 4B as shown in the diagram.

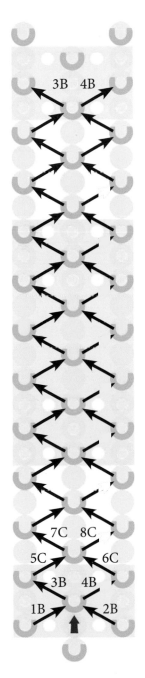

Team Spirit Bracelet
Intermediate

LOOPING THE BANDS

Step 7: Turn the loom around so that the red arrow is pointing toward you.

Step 8: Loop bands 1 and 2 as shown below.

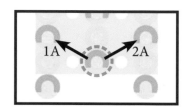

Step 9: Loop bands 1 thru 8 as shown in the diagram to the right.

Step 10: Repeat the pattern 1 thru 8 to the end of the loom. The pattern end on bands 3B - 4B as shown in the diagram.

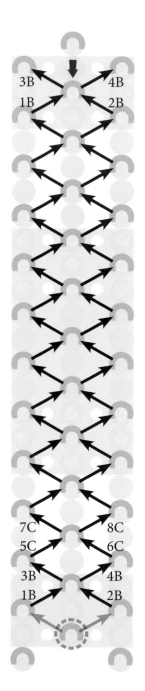

Team Spirit Bracelet
Intermediate

LOOPING THE BANDS

Step 11: Loop bands 1 thru 12.

Step 12: Loop bands 13 thru 24.

Step 13: Tie off with an "A" colored band and go to "Finishing Your Bracelet" on page 12.

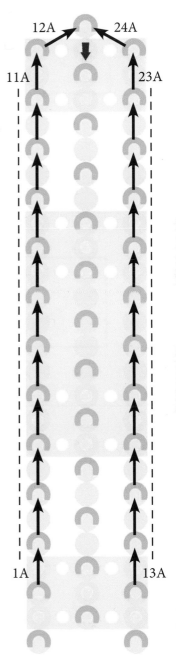

Double Forward Rhombus
Intermediate

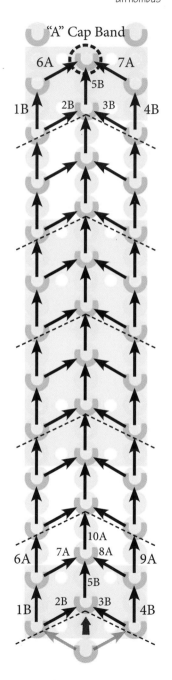

Date First Made:

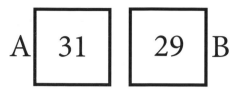

A | 31 | 29 | B

PLACING THE BANDS

Step 1: Turn the loom so that the red arrow is pointing away from you.

Step 2: Place bands 1 and 2 as shown in the diagram below.

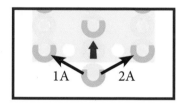

Step 3: Place bands 1 thru 10 as shown in the diagram to the right.

Step 4: Repeat the pattern 1 thru 10 four more times.

Step 5: At the end of the loom, place bands 1 thru 7 as shown in the diagram.

Step 6: Place an "A" colored Cap Band on the last pin as shown in the diagram. See "Making Cap Bands" on page 8.

Double Forward Rhombus
Intermediate

LOOPING THE BANDS

Step 7: Turn the loom around so that the red arrow is pointing toward you.

Step 8: Loop bands 1 thru 10.

Step 9: Repeat the pattern 1 thru 10 four more times.

Step 10: At the end of the loom, loop bands 1 thru 9 as shown in the diagram.

Step 11: Tie off with an "A" colored band and go to "Finishing Your Bracelet" on page 12.

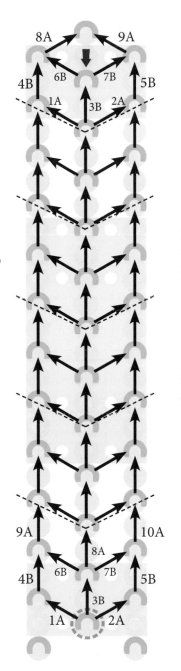

Double Rearward Rhombus
Intermediate

drrhombus

Date First Made:

A | 22

12 | B

C | 28

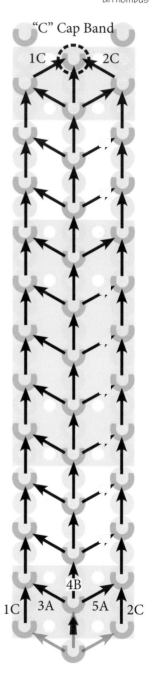

"C" Cap Band

1C   2C

PLACING THE BANDS

Step 1: Turn the loom so that the red arrow is pointing away from you.

Step 2: Place bands 1 thru 3 as shown in the diagram below.

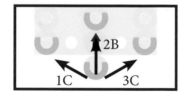

2B

1C   3C

Step 3: Place bands 1 thru 5 as shown in the diagram to the right.

Step 4: Repeat the pattern 1 thru 5 to the end of the loom.

Step 5: Place bands 1 and 2 at the end of the loom as shown in the diagram.

Step 6: Place a "C" colored Cap Band on the last pin as shown in the diagram. See "Making Cap Bands" on page 8.

4B

1C   3A   5A   2C

The Loomatic's Guide - www.LoomaticsGuide.com

Double Rearward Rhombus
Intermediate

LOOPING THE BANDS

Step 7: Turn the loom around so that the red arrov is pointing toward you.

Step 8: Loop bands 1 thru 5 as shown in the diagram below.

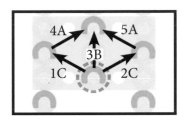

Step 9. Loop bands 1 thru 5 as shown in the diagram to the right.

Step 10: Repeat the pattern 1 thru 5 to the end of the loom.

Step 11: Tie off with a "C" colored band and go to "Finishing Your Bracelet" on page 12.

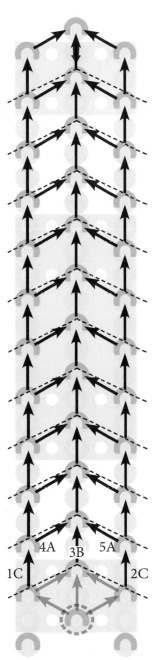

Tulip Tower Bracelet
Intermediate

Date First Made:

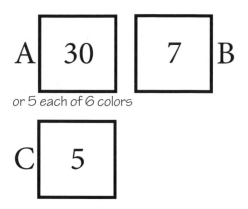

A | 30 | 7 | B

or 5 each of 6 colors

C | 5

PLACING THE BANDS

Step 1: Turn the loom so that the red arrow is pointing away from you.

Step 2: Place bands 1 thru 7.

Step 3: Repeat the pattern 1 thru 7 for the remaining 5 tulips. The last tulip will not have bands 6 & 7 and will stop short of the last pin on the loom.

Step 4: Place a "B" colored Cap Band on the last pin as shown in the diagram. See "Making Cap Bands" on page 8.

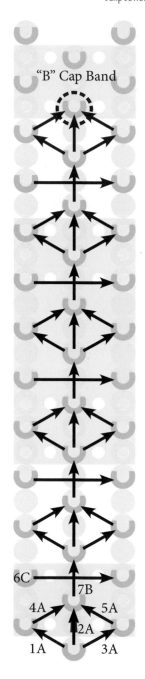

"B" Cap Band

6C   7B
4A   5A
1A   2A   3A

Tulip Tower Bracelet
Intermediate

LOOPING THE BANDS

Step 5: Turn the loom around so that the red arrow is pointing toward you.

Step 6: Loop bands 1 thru 8. See the note below for bands 7 & 8.

Step 7: Repeat the pattern 1 thru 8 to the end of the loom.

Step 8: Tie off with a "B" colored band and go to "Finishing Your Bracelet" on page 12.

Note: The dotted lines, 7 & 8, are the ends of the same band being pulled to the middle pin.

Looping the Tulip Tower

tt_loop

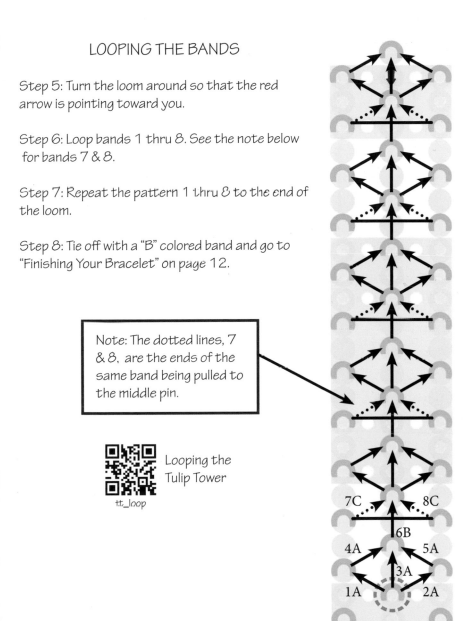

Crossed Hexagon Ring
Intermediate

hexagonring

Date First Made:

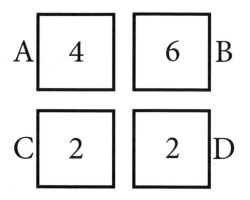

A 4	6 B
C 2	2 D

PLACING THE BANDS

Step 1: Turn the loom so that the red arrow is pointing away from you.

Step 2: Place bands 1 thru 14.

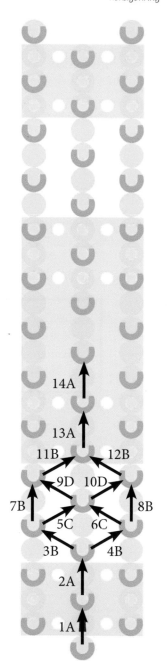

Crossed Hexagon Ring
Intermediate

LOOPING THE BANDS

Step 3: Turn the loom around so that the red arrow is pointing toward you.

Step 4: Using the diagram to the right, loop bands 1 thru 13.

Step 5: Add a C-clip and connect the ends to make a ring. Adjust ring size if needed.

Note: This band is not looped.

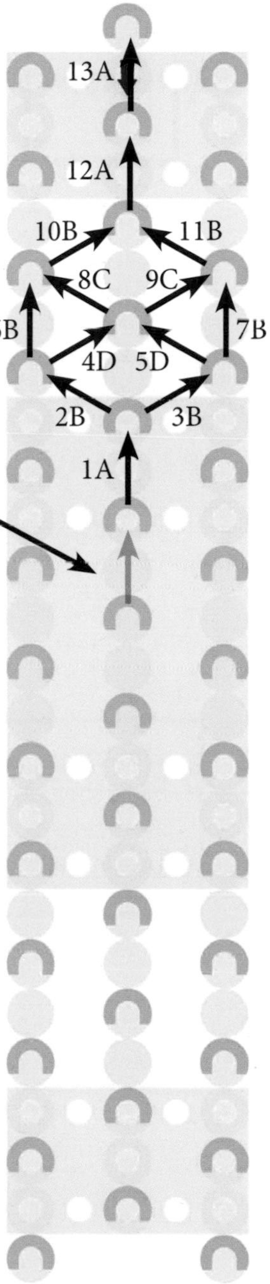

13A
12A
10B   11B
8C   9C
6B   7B
4D   5D
2B   3B
1A

Butterfly Blossom Ring
Intermediate

bbring

Date First Made:

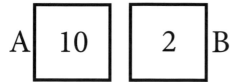

A	10	2	B

PLACING THE BANDS

Step 1: Turn the loom so that the red arrow is pointing away from you.

Step 2: Place bands 1 thru 10.

Step 3: Place bands 11 and 12. They must be twisted to form a "figure 8" before being placed. These two bands are crossed forming an "X" shape.

Note: When placing bands 11 & 12, they can rest on top of the middle pin or be stretched to either side of the middle pin.

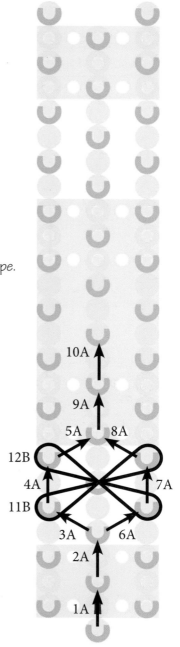

Butterfly Blossom Ring
Intermediate

LOOPING THE BANDS

Step 4: Turn the loom around so that the red arrow is pointing toward you.

Step 5: Loop bands 1 thru 9. See the note below.

Step 6: Add a C-clip and connect the ends to make a ring. Adjust ring size if needed.

Note: This band is not looped.

Note: Make certain that you loop through the ends of the figure 8 bands. Use the back of the hook to pull the figure 8 away while you grab the bottom "A" band.

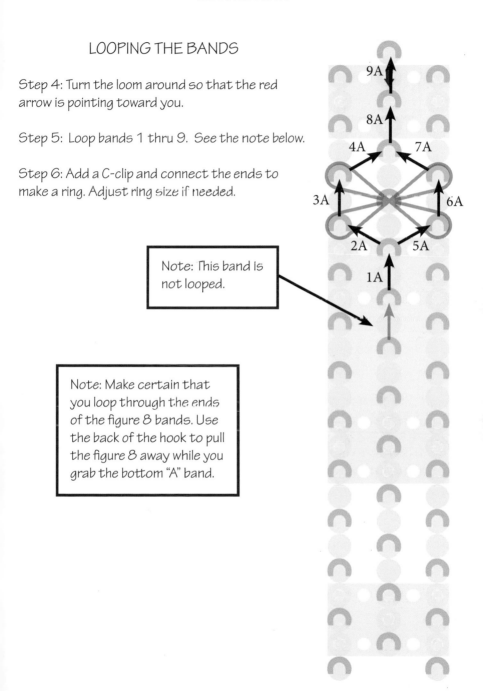

Sweetheart Bracelet
Intermediate

Date First Made:

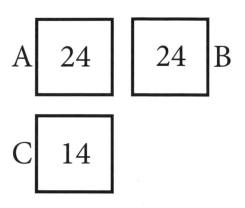

A 24   24 B

C 14

PLACING THE BANDS

Step 1: Convert the loom from an "offset" to a "rectangle" configuration. To learn how to do this, see "Loom Configurations" on page 182.

Step 2: Turn the loom so that the red arrow is pointing away from you.

Step 3: Place bands 1 thru 5. On this design, do not push the bands down on the pins. If you do, looping the bands will be difficult.

Step 4: Repeat the pattern 1 thru 5 to the end of the loom.

Step 5: Place a "C" colored Cap Band on the last pin as shown in the diagram. See "Making Cap Bands" on page 8.

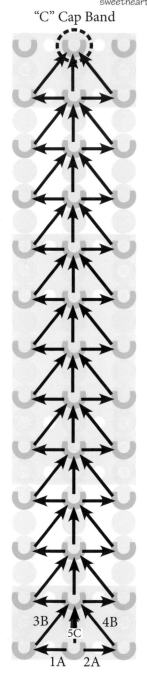

"C" Cap Band

3B   4B

5C

1A   2A

Sweetheart Bracelet
Intermediate

LOOPING THE BANDS

Step 6: Turn the loom around so that the red arrow is pointing toward you.

Step 7: Loop the bands 1 thru 5.

Step 8: Repeat the pattern 1 thru 5 to the end of the loom.

Step 9: Tie off with an "C" colored band and go to "Finishing Your Bracelet" on page 12.

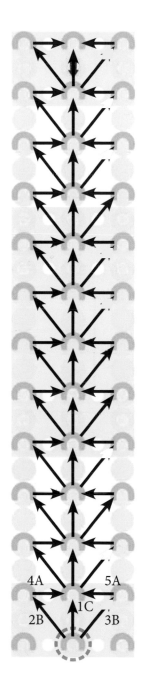

Heart Bracelet
Intermediate

Date First Made:

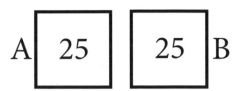

A| 25 | 25 |B

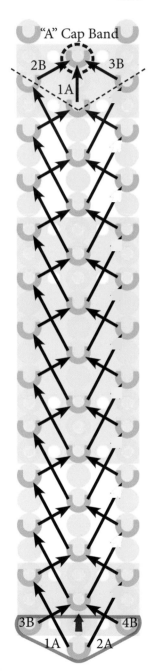

"A" Cap Band

2B   3B

1A

PLACING THE BANDS

Step 1: Turn the loom so that the red arrow is pointing away from you.

Step 2: Place band 1 as shown in the diagram below.

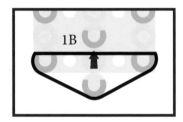

1B

Step 3: Place bands 1 thru 4 as shown in the diagram to the right.

Step 4: Repeat the pattern 1 thru 4 to the second to last row. Stop at the dashed line as shown on the diagram.

Step 5: Place bands 1 thru 3 shown above the dashed line.

Step 6: Place an "A" colored Cap Band on the last pin as shown in the diagram. See "Making Cap Bands" on page 8.

3B   4B

1A   2A

Heart Bracelet
Intermediate

LOOPING THE BANDS

Step 7: Turn the loom around so that the red arrow is pointing toward you.

Step 8: Loop bands 1 thru 3 at the beginning of the loom as shown below.

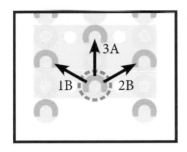

Step 9: Loop bands 1 thru 4 as shown in the diagram to the right.

Step 10: Repeat the pattern 1 thru 4 to the end of the loom.

Step 11: Loop the corners of triangle band to the center pin as shown by the dotted arrows 1B & 2B.

Step 12: Tie off with a "B" colored band and go to "Finishing Your Bracelet" on page 12.

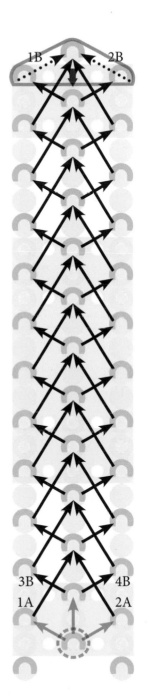

Serpentine Bracelet
Intermediate

Date First Made:

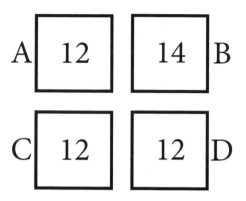

A	12	14	B
C	12	12	D

PLACING THE BANDS

Step 1: Turn the loom so that the red arrow is pointing away from you.

Step 2: Place bands 1 thru 8.

Step 3: Repeat the pattern 1 thru 8 to the end of the loom.

Step 4: Place a "B" colored Cap Band on the last pin as shown in the diagram. See "Making Cap Bands" on page 8.

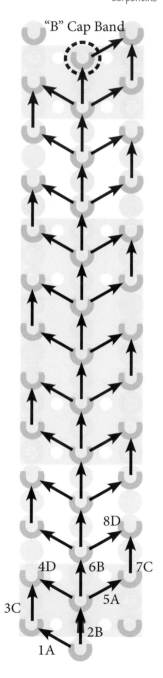

"B" Cap Band

8D

4D   6B   7C

3C   5A

2B

1A

Serpentine Bracelet
Intermediate

LOOPING THE BANDS

Step 5: Turn the loom around so that the red arrow is pointing toward you.

Step 6: Loop bands 1 thru 8.

Step 7: Repeat the pattern 1 thru 8 to the end of the loom.

Step 8: Tie off with a "B" colored band and go to "Finishing Your Bracelet" on page 12.

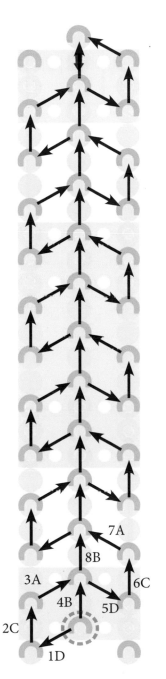

Butterfly Blossoms Bracelet
Intermediate

bfblossom

Date First Made:

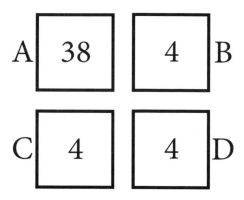

A $\boxed{38}$	$\boxed{4}$ B
C $\boxed{4}$	$\boxed{4}$ D

PLACING THE BANDS

Step 1: Turn the loom so that the red arrow is pointing away from you.

Step 2: Place bands 1 thru 6.

Step 3: Repeat the pattern 1 thru 6 to the end of the loom.

Step 4: Place an "A" colored Cap Band on the last pin as shown in the diagram. See "Making Cap Bands" on page 8.

Things to try

Try a different color for each hexagon.

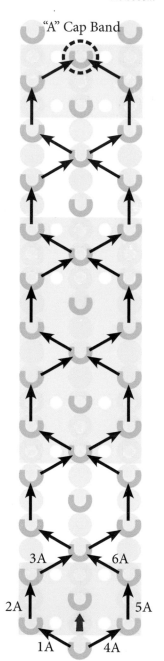

"A" Cap Band

3A   6A

2A   5A

1A   4A

Butterfly Blossoms Bracelet
Intermediate

PLACING THE BANDS

Step 5: Place bands 1 thru 6. As you place each band, twist it to form a figure 8 as shown in the diagram. Notice that you are skipping a row of pins between each band.

Note: When placing the figure 8 bands, they can rest on top of the middle pin or be stretched to either side of the middle pin.

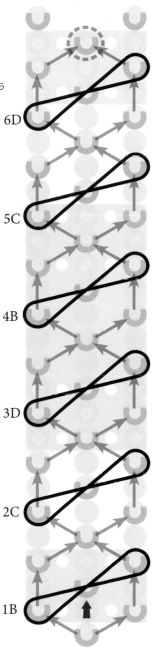

Butterfly Blossoms Bracelet
Intermediate

PLACING THE BANDS

Step 6: Place bands 1 thru 6. As you place each band, twist it to form a figure 8 as shown in the diagram. With this set of bands you are forming an "X" inside each hexagon.

Notice how the orange & blue bands are twisted into a figure 8 and form an "X" over the center pin.

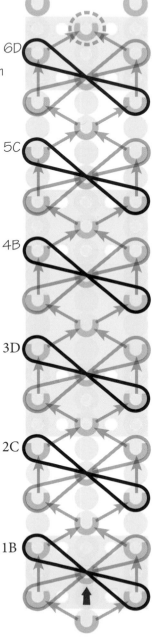

Butterfly Blossoms Bracelet
Intermediate

LOOPING THE BANDS

Step 7: Turn the loom around so that the red arrow is pointing toward you.

Step 8: Loop bands 1 thru 6. See the note below.

Step 9: Repeat the pattern 1 thru 6 to the end of the loom.

Step 10: Tie off with an "A" colored band and go to "Finishing Your Bracelet" on page 12.

Note: Make certain that you loop through the ends of the figure 8 bands. Use the back of the hook to pull the figure 8 away while you grab the bottom "A" band.

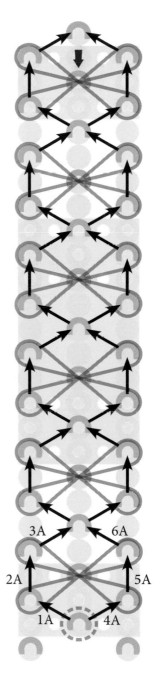

Diamond with Rings Bracelet
Intermediate

diamondrings

Date First Made:

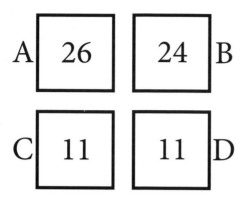

A | 26 | 24 | B

C | 11 | 11 | D

PLACING THE BANDS

Step 1: Turn the loom so that the red arrow is pointing away from you.

Step 2: Place bands 1 thru 8.

Step 3: Continue the pattern 1 thru 8 to the end of the loom.

Step 4: Place an "A" colored Cap Band on the last pin as shown in the diagram. See "Making Cap Bands" on page 8.

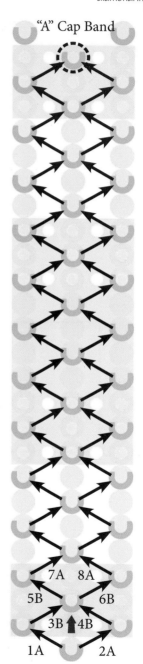

"A" Cap Band

7A 8A
5B 6B
3B 4B
1A 2A

Diamond with Rings Bracelet
Intermediate

PLACING THE BANDS

Step 5: Place bands 1 thru 11. Notice how these bands are placed around three pins to form a triangle.

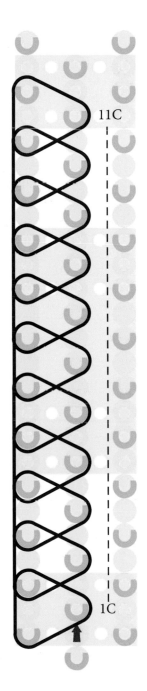

11C

1C

Diamond with Rings Bracelet
Intermediate

PLACING THE BANDS

Step 6: Place bands 1 thru 11. Notice how these bands are placed around three pins to form a triangle.

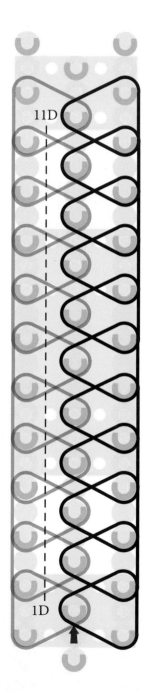

11D

1D

Diamond with Rings Bracelet
Intermediate

LOOPING THE BANDS

Step 7: Turn the loom around so that the red arrow is pointing toward you.

Step 8: Loop bands 1 thru 8. You will not be looping the triangle bands, but you must loop through them when pulling the 1 thru 8 bands.

Step 9: Continue the pattern 1 thru 8 to the end of the loom.

Step 10: Tie off with an "A" colored band and go to "Finishing Your Bracelet" on page 12.

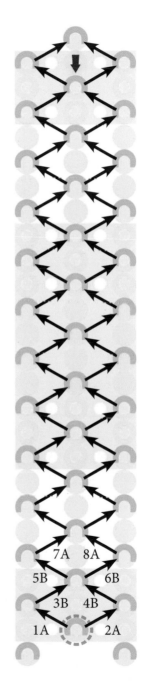

Triple Single with Rings
Intermediate

Date First Made:

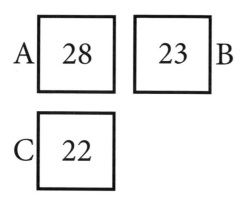

A | 28   23 | B

C | 22

PLACING THE BANDS

Step 1: Turn the loom so that the red arrow is pointing away from you.

Step 2: Place bands 1 thru 13.

Step 3: Place bands 14 thru 26.

Step 4: Place bands 27 thru 38.

Step 5: Place an "A" colored Cap Band on the last pin as shown in the diagram. See "Making Cap Bands" on page 8.

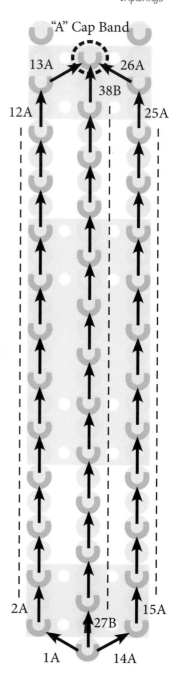

Triple Single with Rings
Intermediate

PLACING THE BANDS

Step 6: Place bands 1 thru 11. Notice how these bands are placed around three pins to form a triangle.

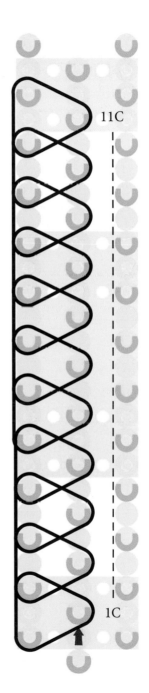

11C

1C

Triple Single with Rings
Intermediate

PLACING THE BANDS

Step 7: Place bands 1 thru 11. Notice how these bands are placed around three pins to form a triangle.

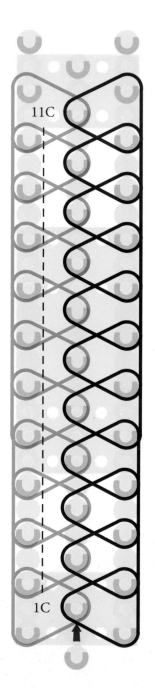

11C

1C

Triple Single with Rings
Intermediate

PLACING THE BANDS

Step 8: Push all of the bands down on the pins making room for more bands on top.

Step 9: Place bands 1 thru 11. Notice how these bands are placed around three pins to form a triangle.

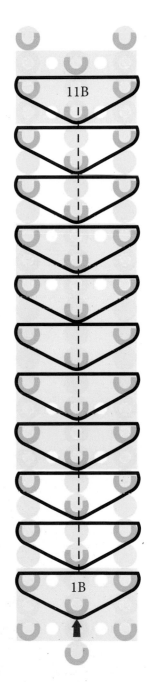

Triple Single with Rings
Intermediate

LOOPING THE BANDS

Step 10: Turn the loom around so that the red arrow is pointing toward you.

Step 11: Loop bands 1 thru 12.

Step 12: Loop bands 13 thru 25.

Step 13: Loop bands 26 thru 38.

Step 14: Tie off with an "A" colored band and go to "Finishing Your Bracelet" on page 12.

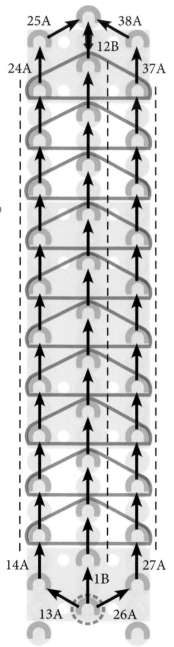

Raindrops Bracelet
Intermediate

Date First Made:

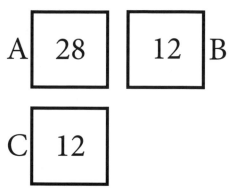

A | 28 | 12 | B

C | 12

PLACING THE BANDS

Step 1: Turn the loom so that the red arrow is pointing away from you.

Step 2: Place bands 1 thru 4 as shown in the diagram below. Note that bands 3 and 4 are placed one on top of the other. Make sure you always place the "B" colored band first.

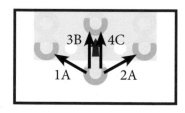

Step 3: Place bands 1 thru 4 as shown in the diagram to the right.

Step 4: Repeat the pattern 1 thru 4 nine more times.

Step 5: IMPORTANT! At the end of the loom, place bands 1 thru 6 **as shown in the diagram**.

Step 6: Place an "A" colored Cap Band as shown.

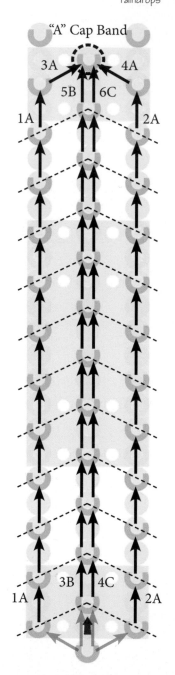

"A" Cap Band

Raindrops Bracelet
Intermediate

LOOPING THE BANDS

Step 7: Turn the loom around so that the red arrow is pointing toward you.

Step 8: Loop bands 1 thru 6 as shown in the diagram below.

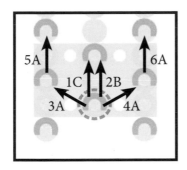

Step 9: Loop bands 1 thru 4 as shown in the diagram to the right.

Step 10: Repeat the pattern 1 thru 4 nine more times.

Step 11: At the end of the loom, loop bands 1 thru 4 as shown in the diagram.

Step 12: Tie off with an "A" colored band and go to "Finishing Your Bracelet" on page 12.

Looping
Raindrows

rain_loop

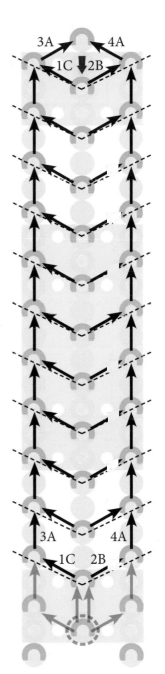

The Rectangle Bracelet
Intermediate
Submitted by Lyndsey West
Reno, NV

Date First Made:

rectangle

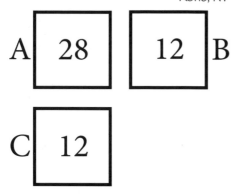

A | 28

12 | B

C | 12

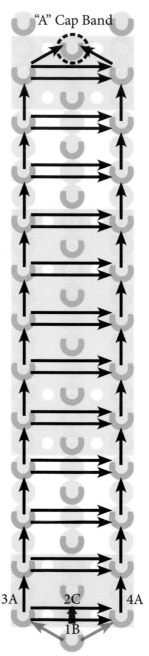

"A" Cap Band

"A" Cap Band

3A   2C   4A

1B

PLACING THE BANDS

Step 1: Turn the loom so that the red arrow is pointing away from you.

Step 2: Place bands 1 & 2 as shown below.

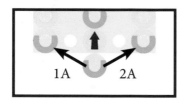

1A   2A

Step 3: Place bands 1 thru 4 as shown in the diagram to the right.

Step 4: Repeat the pattern 1 thru 4 to the end of the loom. On the last row, bands 3 & 4 end at the center pin as shown in the diagram.

Step 5: Place an "A" colored cap band on the last pin as shown in the diagram. To learn how to make a cap band, see "Making Cap Bands" on page 8.

The Rectangle Bracelet
Intermediate

LOOPING THE BANDS

Step 6: Turn the loom around so that the red arrow is pointing toward you.

Step 7: Loop bands 1 and 2 as shown below.

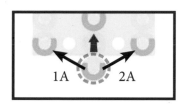

Step 8: Loop bands 1 thru 4 as shown in the diagram to the right. Notice that the "B" colored band is looped to the left and the "C" colored band is looped to the right.

Step 9: Repeat the pattern 1 thru 4 to the end of the loom. On the last row, bands 3 & 4 are looped to the center pin as shown in the diagram.

Step 10: Tie off with an "A" colored band and go to "Finishing Your Bracelet" on page 12.

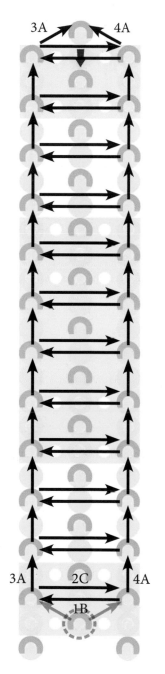

Rose Garden Bracelet
Intermediate

Date First Made:

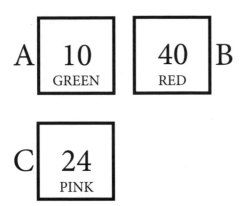

A | **10** GREEN   **40** RED | B

C | **24** PINK

For this bracelet two chains will be made and attached together.

PLACING THE BANDS

Step 1: Turn the loom so that the red arrow is pointing away from you.

Step 2: Place bands 1 thru 9.

Step 3: Repeat the pattern 1 thru 9 for the remaining 3 roses.

Step 4: Place an "A" colored Cap Band on the last pin as shown in the diagram. See "Making Cap Bands" on page 8.

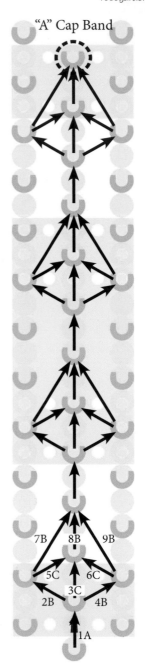

"A" Cap Band

7B   8B   9B

5C   6C

3C

2B   4B

1A

Rose Garden Bracelet
Intermediate

LOOPING THE BANDS

Step 5: Turn the loom around so that the red arrow is pointing toward you.

Step 6: Loop bands 1 thru 9.

Step 7: Repeat the pattern 1 thru 9 to the end of the loom.

Step 8: Place your hook thru the last "A" colored band and move the band to the thickest part of the hook. Remove the bracelet from the loom. Set the hook, with the bracelet attached, aside.

Things to try

After your bracelet has been removed from the loom, tie a green band around each of the "A" bands to create "leaves".

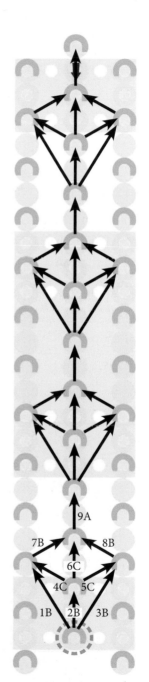

Rose Garden Bracelet
Intermediate

PLACING MORE BANDS

Step 9: Turn the loom so that the red arrow is pointing away from you.

Step 10: Place bands 1 thru 9.

Step 11: Repeat the pattern 1 thru 9 for the remaining 3 roses.

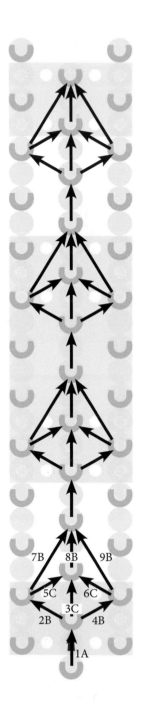

Rose Garden Bracelet
Intermediate

LOOPING MORE BANDS

Step 12: Turn the loom around so that the red arrow is pointing toward you.

Step 13: Stretch the "A" band that is around your hook around the three pins on the loom as shown in the photo below.

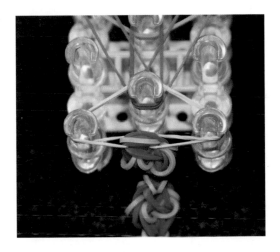

Step 14: Loop bands 1 thru 9.

Step 15: Repeat the pattern 1 thru 9 to the end of the loom.

Step 16: Attach a C-clip to the last band looped.

Step 17: Remove the bracelet from the loom and connect the two ends together with the C-clip.

This triangle band is the green triangle band shown in the photo above.

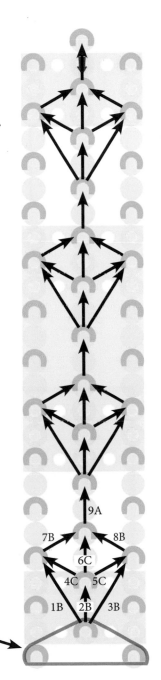

Upsy Daisy Twistzy Wistzy

Intermediate

Date First Made:

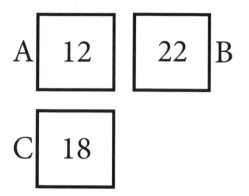

A | 12   22 | B

C | 18

PLACING THE BANDS

Step 1: Turn the loom so that the red arrow is pointing away from you.

Step 2: Place bands 1 thru 12. Notice that the first & last bands form a triangle shape, the others form a diamond shape.

Things to try

Instead of alternating "C" and "B" bands, place 2 rows of "C" bands and then 2 rows of "B" bands, etc.

Try placing the bands in Step 2 in rainbow order: red - orange - yellow - green - blue - purple.

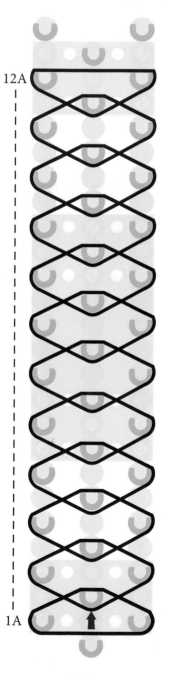

12A

1A

Upsy Daisy Twistzy Wistzy
Intermediate

PLACING THE BANDS

Step 3: Place bands 1 and 2 as shown in the diagram below.

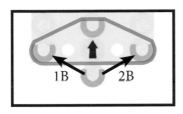

Step 4: Place bands 1 thru 6 as shown in the diagram to the right.

Step 5: Repeat the pattern 1 thru 6 to the end of the loom.

Step 6: Place a "B" colored Cap Band on the last pin as shown in the diagram. See "Making Cap Bands" on page 8.

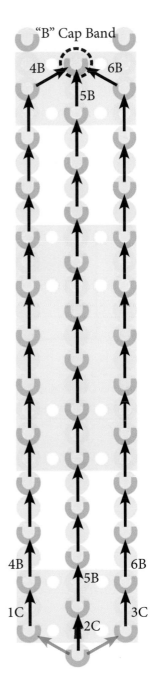

Upsy Daisy Twistzy Wistzy
Intermediate

LOOPING THE BANDS

Step 7: Turn the loom around so that the red arrow is pointing toward you.

Step 8: Loop bands 1 thru 5 as shown below. Band 4A & 5A, shown by the dotted arrow, are the corners of the triangle, and need to be looped to the center pin.

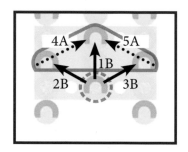

Step 9: Loop bands 1 thru 6 shown in the diagram to the right. Bands 2, 3, 5, & 6 are the corners of the diamonds being looped to the center.

Step 10: Repeat the pattern 1 thru 6 to the end of the loom.

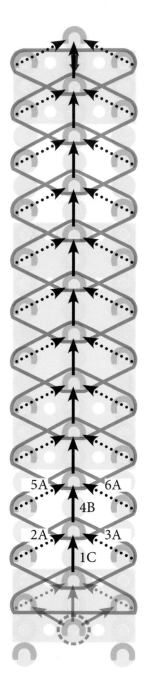

Upsy Daisy Twistzy Wistzy
Intermediate

LOOPING THE BANDS

Step 11: Loop bands 1 thru 12. The bands will alternate between "C" and "B" color.

Step 12: Loop bands 13 thru 24. The bands will alternate between "C" and "B" color.

Step 13: Tie off with a "B" colored band and go to "Finishing Your Bracelet" on page 12.

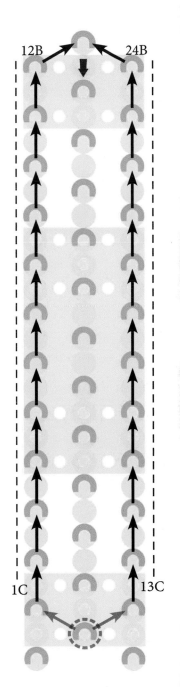

Add your Rainbow Loom Creations to Headbands!

Examples of headbands that you can make with the Rainbow Bloom Charm, Butterfly Blossoms Bracelet, Hibiscus Charm, and the Star Burst Bracelet.

Advanced Designs

Zig Zag Bracelet
Advanced

Date First Made:

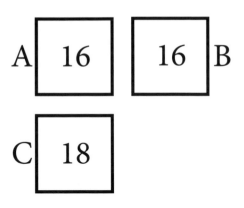

"C" Cap Band

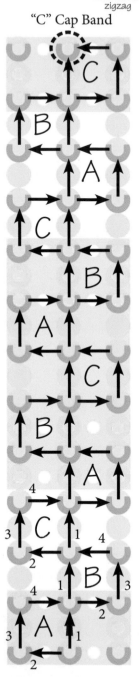

PLACING THE BANDS

Step 1: Convert the loom from an "offset" to a "rectangle" configuration. To learn how to do this, see "Loom Configurations" on page 182.

Step 2: Turn the loom so that the red arrow is pointing away from you.

Step 3: Using the diagram to the right and the patterns below, form the 12 squares shown in the diagram starting from the bottom left square and moving up. The order the bands are placed depends on whether the square is on the left side of the loom or the right side. Alternate colors as you move up the loom: A - B - C.

Step 4: Place "C" colored Cap Band as shown.

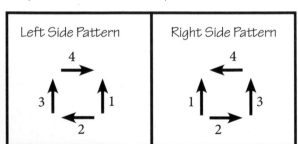

118   The Loomatic's Guide - www.LoomaticsGuide.com

Zig Zag Bracelet
Advanced

LOOPING THE BANDS

Step 5: Turn the loom around so that the red arrow is pointing toward you.

Step 6: Loop each square, one at a time, starting from the bottom left and moving up the loom. Loop the bands following the diagram to the right and the pattern guide below.

Step 7: Tie off with a "C" colored band and go to "Finishing Your Bracelet" on page 12.

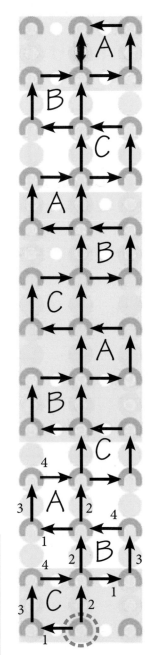

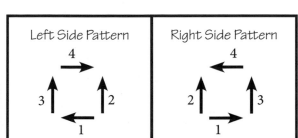

Starfish Bracelet
Advanced

Date First Made:

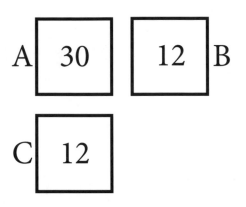

A 30   12 B

C 12

PLACING THE BANDS

Step 1: Convert the loom from an "offset" to a "rectangle" configuration.

Step 2: Turn the loom so that the red arrow is pointing away from you.

Step 3: Place bands 1 and 2 as shown below.

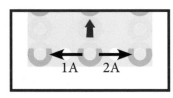

Step 4: Place bands 1 thru 16 as shown in the diagram to the right.

Step 5: Repeat the pattern 1 thru 16 two more times.

Step 6: Place bands 1 & 2 at end of loom as shown in the diagram to the right.

Step 7: Place an "A" colored Cap Band on the last pin as shown in the diagram.

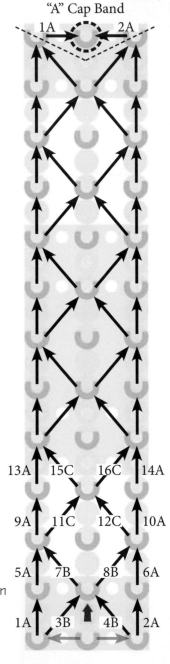

"A" Cap Band

Starfish Bracelet
Advanced

LOOPING THE BANDS

Step 8: Turn the loom so that the red arrow is pointing toward you.

Step 9: Loop bands 1 and 2 as shown below.

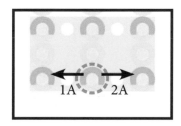

Step 10: Loop bands 1 thru 16 as shown in the diagram to the right.

Step 11: Repeat the pattern 1 thru 16 two more times.

Step 12: At the end of the loom, loop bands 1 and 2 to the center pin as shown below and in the diagram to the right.

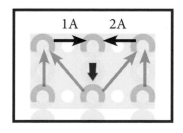

Step 13: Tie off with an "A" colored band and go to "Finishing Your Bracelet" on page 12.

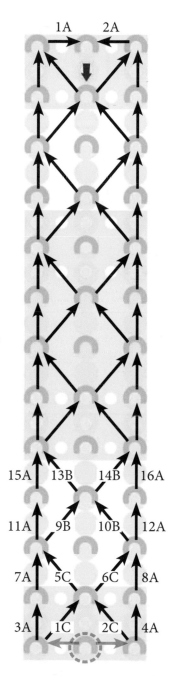

Twistzy Wistzy Bracelet
Advanced

Date First Made:

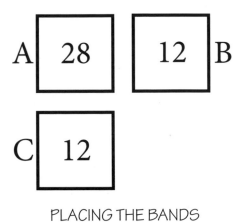

A | 28 | | 12 | B

C | 12

PLACING THE BANDS

Step 1: Turn the loom so that the red arrow is pointing away from you.

Step 2: Place bands 1 thru 13.

Step 3: Place bands 14 thru 26.

Step 4: Place bands 27 thru 38.

Step 5: Place an "A" colored Cap Band on the last pin as shown in the diagram.

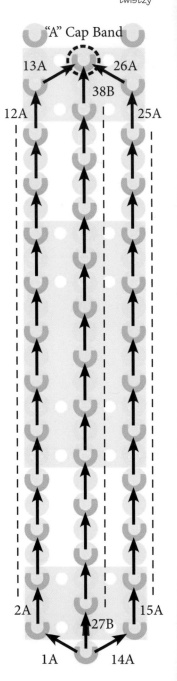

Twistzy Wistzy Bracelet
Advanced

PLACING THE BANDS

Step 6: Push all of the bands down on the pins.

Step 7: Place triangular shaped band 1.

Step 8: Place diamond shaped bands 2 thru 11.

Step 9: Place triangular shaped band 12.

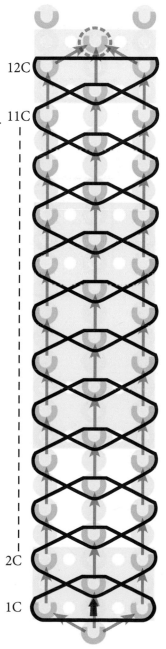

Twistzy Wistzy Bracelet
Advanced

LOOPING THE BANDS

Step 10: Turn the loom around so that the red arrow is pointing toward you.

Step 11: Loop bands 1 thru 5 as shown below. Bands 4C & 5C, as shown by the dotted arrows, are the corners of the triangle, and need to be looped to the center pin.

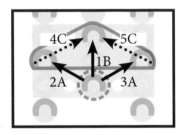

Step 12: Loop bands 1 thru 5 as shown in the diagram to the right. Bands 4 & 5 are the corners of the diamond being looped to the center pin.

Step 13: Repeat the pattern 1 thru 5 to the end of the loom.

Step 14: After looping the last triangle band to the center pin, loop bands 1 & 2 to the center as shown at the top of the diagram.

Step 15: Tie off with an "A" colored band and go to "Finishing Your Bracelet" on page 12.

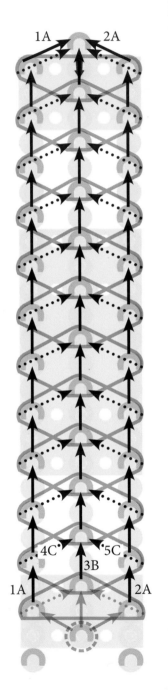

Ladybug Bracelet
Advanced

Date First Made:

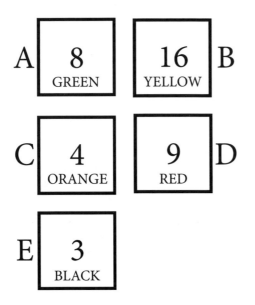

A	8 GREEN	16 YELLOW	B
C	4 ORANGE	9 RED	D
E	3 BLACK		

PLACING THE BANDS

Step 1: Turn the loom so that the red arrow is pointing away from you.

Step 2: Following the diagram to the right, place bands 1 thru 38.

Step 3: Place an "A" colored Cap Band on the last pin as shown in the diagram. See "Making Cap Bands" on page 8.

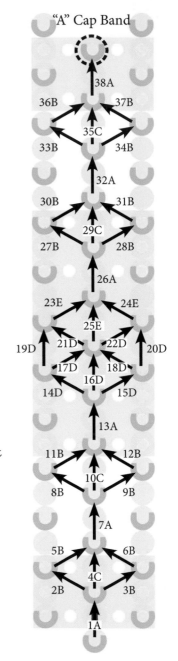

Ladybug Bracelet
Advanced

LOOPING THE BANDS

Step 4: Turn the loom around so that the red arrow is pointing toward you.

Step 5: Loop bands 1 thru 38.

Step 6: Tie off with an "A" colored band and go to "Finishing Your Bracelet" on page 12.

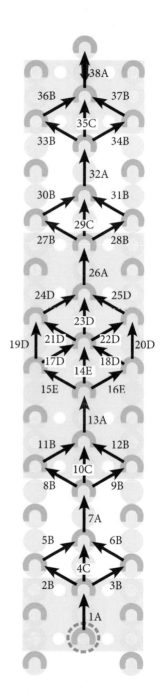

Honey Bee Bracelet
Advanced

Date First Made:

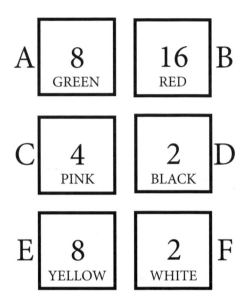

A [8 GREEN]   [16 RED] B

C [4 PINK]   [2 BLACK] D

E [8 YELLOW]   [2 WHITE] F

PLACING THE BANDS

Step 1: Turn the loom so that the red arrow is pointing away from you.

Step 2: Place bands 1 thru 15. It is very important that the bands be placed in the exact order shown otherwise your bracelet will fall apart.

The colors listed above are suggested colors.

A = Color of stem
B = Color of flowers
C = Flower highlight

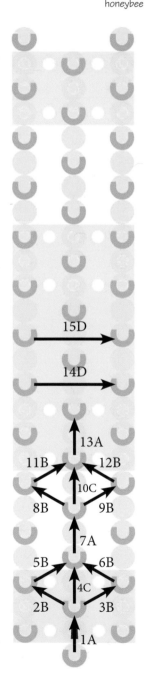

Honey Bee Bracelet
Advanced

PLACING THE BANDS

Step 3: Turn the loom around so that the red arrow is pointing toward you.

Step 4: Place bands 1 thru 21.

Step 5: Place an "A" colored Cap Band on the last pin as shown in the diagram. See "Making Cap Bands" on page 8.

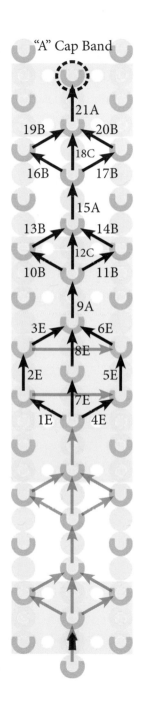

"A" Cap Band

21A
19B   20B
18C
16B   17B

15A
13B   14B
12C
10B   11B

9A
3E   6E
8E
2E   5E
7E
1E   4E

Honey Bee Bracelet
Advanced

PLACING THE BANDS

Step 5: Place triangle shaped bands 1 and 2 from the center of the hexagon as shown.

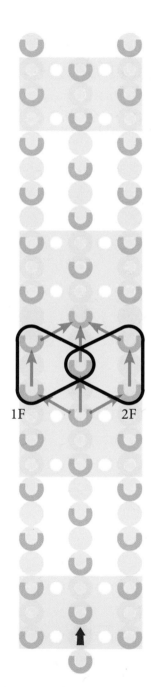

Honey Bee Bracelet
Advanced

LOOPING THE BANDS

Step 6: Loop bands 1 thru 20.

Step 7: Loop bands 21 thru 25. Make sure you do these in the right order. See the note below.

Step 8: Loop bands 26 thru 38.

Step 9: Tie off with an "A" colored band and go to "Finishing Your Bracelet" on page 12.

Note: The dotted line bands do not loop back on themselves like most bands do.

For bands 21 thru 24, you loop both ends of the "D" colored bands from the outside pin to the middle pin.

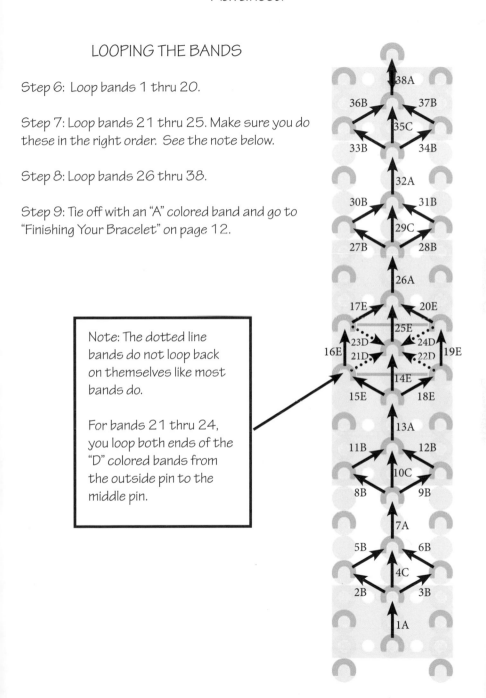

Star Burst Bracelet

Advanced
Submitted by Danielle Wilhelm
Sylvania, OH

starburst

Date First Made:

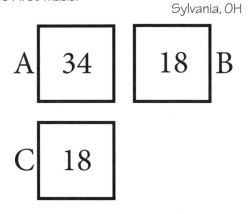

A | 34

18 | B

C | 18

PLACING THE BANDS

Step 1: Turn the loom so that the red arrow is pointing away from you.

Step 2: Place bands 1 thru 13.

Step 3: Place bands 14 thru 26.

Tip

If you are having difficulty looping this bracelet, try using six different colored bands in each Star Burst until you get the hang of it.

You may also find it easier to use a different colored Cap Band for each Star Burst.

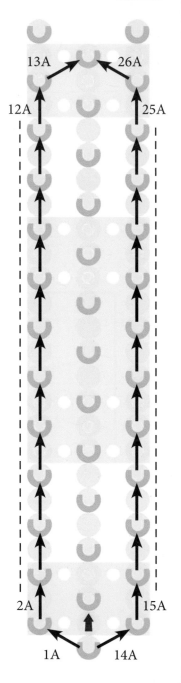

Star Burst Bracelet
Advanced

PLACING THE BANDS

Step 4: Place bands 1 thru 6. See the note below.

Step 5: Place bands 7 thru 12.

Step 6: Repeat Step 4 & 5 for the remaining 4 Star Bursts.

Note: When placing the bands for the Star Bursts, the order in which they are placed is very important. The first band is placed in the 2 o'clock position and then you rotate clockwise until you reach the 12 o'clock position.

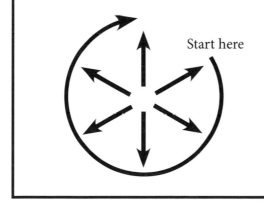

Start here

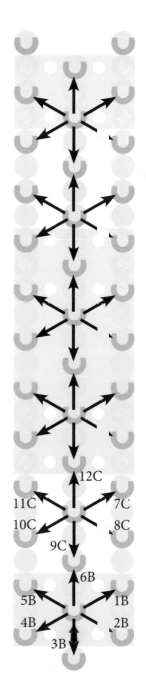

Star Burst Bracelet
Advanced

PLACING THE BANDS

Step 7: Place Cap Bands 1 thru 6.

Step 8: Place an "A" colored Cap Band on the last pin as shown in the diagram. See "Making Cap Bands" on page 8.

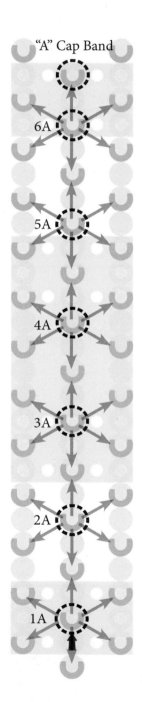

"A" Cap Band

Star Burst Bracelet
Advanced

LOOPING THE BANDS

Step 9: Turn the loom around so that the red arrow is pointing toward you.

Step 10: Loop bands 1 thru 6. It is very important to loop the bands in the right order and in the right direction. See note below.

Step 11: Loop bands 7 thru 12.

Step 12: Repeat the pattern 1 thru 12 to the end of the loom.

Note: When looping the Star Burst, you start at the 6 o'clock position and then rotate counter clockwise.

Notice that the first band is looped toward the center of the Star Burst, while the other 5 bands are looped toward the outside of the Star Burst. (see the direction of the arrows in the diagram)

Start here

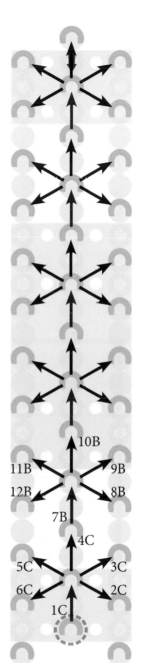

Star Burst Bracelet
Advanced

LOOPING THE BANDS

Step 13: Loop bands 1 thru 13.

Step 12: Loop bands 14 thru 26.

Step 13: Tie off with an "A" colored band and go to "Finishing Your Bracelet" on page 12.

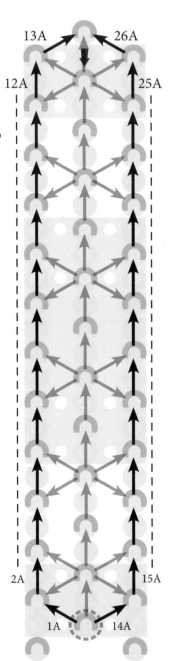

Things to try

Experiment with different colors for each of the Star Bursts.

Try adding pony beads to every other Star Burst.

Make the Cap Bands the same color as the Star Burst.

Flower Power Bracelet
Advanced

Date First Made:

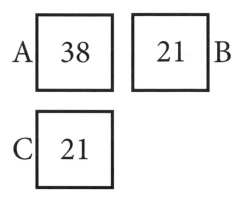

A | 38   21 | B

C | 21

PLACING THE BANDS

Step 1: Place the loom so that the red arrow is pointing away from you.

Step 2: Place bands 1 thru 6.

Step 3: Repeat the pattern 1 thru 6 to end of the loom.

Things to try

Try making each flower a different color.

Try making the bracelet with 4 hexagons separated by a single band between them.

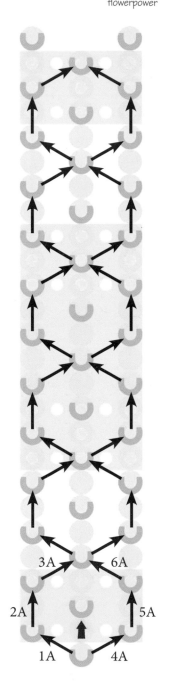

Flower Power Bracelet
Advanced

PLACING THE BANDS

Step 4: Place bands 1 thru 6.

Step 5: Place bands 7 thru 12.

Step 6: Repeat steps 4 & 5 for the remaining 4 flowers.

Note: When placing the bands for the flowers, the order in which they are placed is very important. The first band is placed in the 2 o'clock position and then you rotate clockwise until you reach the 12 o'clock position.

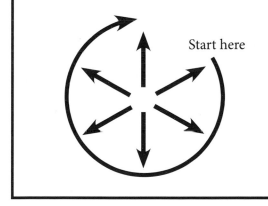

Start here

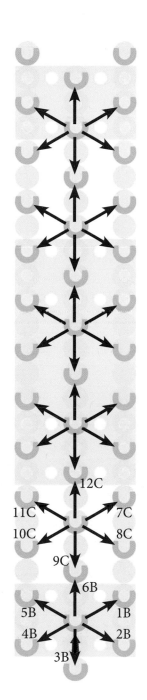

Flower Power Bracelet
Advanced

PLACING THE BANDS

Step 7: Place Cap Bands 1 thru 6.

Step 8: Place an "A" colored Cap Band on the last pin as shown in the diagram. See "Making Cap Bands" on page 8.

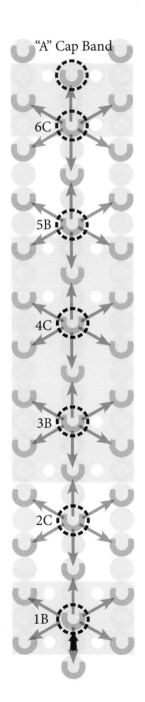

"A" Cap Band

6C

5B

4C

3B

2C

1B

Tip

If you are having difficulty looping this bracelet, try using six different colored bands in each flower until you get the hang of it.

You may also find it easier to use a different colored Cap Band for each flower.

Flower Power Bracelet
Advanced

LOOPING THE BANDS

Step 9: Turn the loom around so that the red arrow is pointing toward you.

Step 10: Loop bands 1 thru 6. It is very important to loop the bands in the right order and in the right direction. See the note below.

Step 11: Loop bands 7 thru 12.

Step 12: Repeat the pattern 1 thru 12 to the end of the loom.

Note: When looping the flowers, you start at the 6 o'clock position and then rotate counter clockwise.

Notice that all bands are looped outward from the center of the flower.

Start here

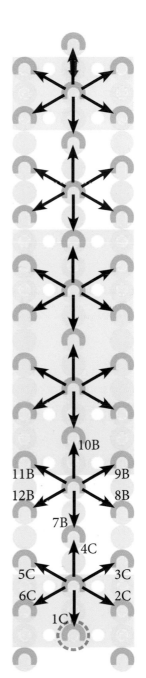

Flower Power Bracelet
Advanced

LOOPING THE BANDS

Step 13: Loop bands 1 thru 6.

Step 14: Repeat the pattern 1 thru 6 to the end of the loom.

Step 15: Tie off with an "A" colored band and go to "Finishing Your Bracelet" on page 12.

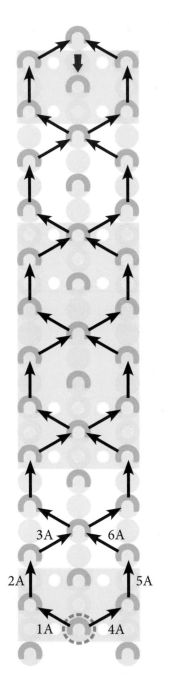

> ## Tip
>
> If you are having difficulty looping this bracelet, try using a different color band for each petal of the flower until you get the hang of it.
>
> You may also find it easier to use a different colored Cap Band for each flower.

Rainbow Blooms Bracelet
Advanced

Date First Made:

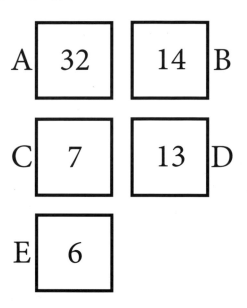

A | 32   14 | B

C | 7   13 | D

E | 6

PLACING THE BANDS

Step 1: Turn the loom so that the red arrow is pointing away from you.

Step 2: Place bands 1 thru 6. See the diagram below.

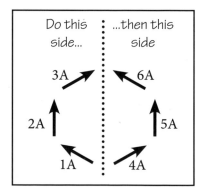

Do this side...   ...then this side

3A   6A

2A   5A

1A   4A

Step 3: Repeat the pattern 1 thru 6 four more times.

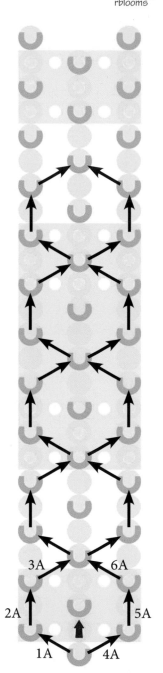

Rainbow Blooms Bracelet
Advanced

PLACING THE BANDS

Step 4: Place bands 1 thru 18. Make sure you place them in the right order. See the note below.

Note: When placing the bands for the blooms, the order in which they are placed is very important. The first band is placed in the 2 o'clock position and then you rotate clockwise until you reach the 12 o'clock position.

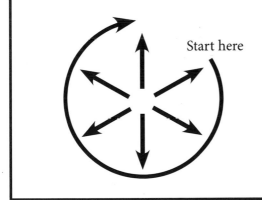

Start here

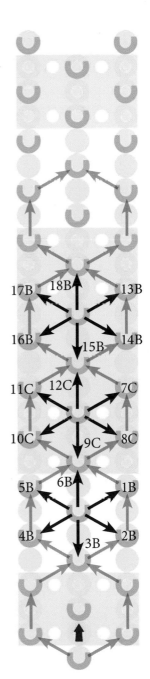

Rainbow Blooms Bracelet
Advanced

PLACING THE BANDS

Step 5: Place bands 1 thru 22. When placing the hexagons, make sure you place them in the right order as shown in the diagram below.

Note bands 7, 14, 21, and 22 are Cap Bands.

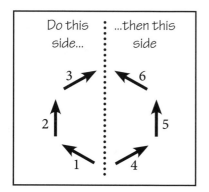

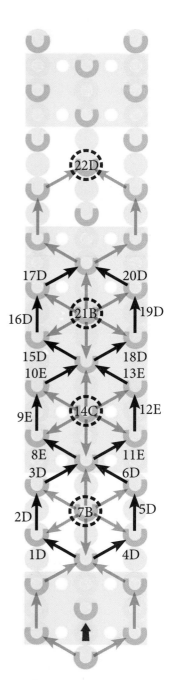

Rainbow Blooms Bracelet
Advanced

LOOPING THE BANDS

Step 6: Turn the loom around so that the red arrow is pointing toward you.

Step 7: Loop bands 1 thru 18.

Note: When looping the blooms, you start at the 6 o'clock position and then rotate counter clockwise.

Notice that all of the bands are looped outward from the center of the bloom.

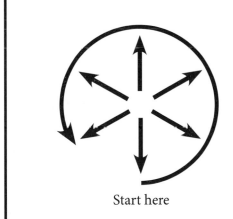

Start here

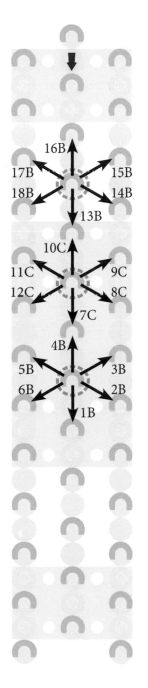

Rainbow Blooms Bracelet
Advanced

LOOPING THE BANDS

Step 8: Loop bands 1 thru 6. Make sure you loop them in the right order.

Step 9: Repeat the pattern 1 thru 6 four more times.

Step 10: Tie off with an "A" colored band and go to "Finishing Your Bracelet" on page 12.

Note: This bracelet requires adjustment after it is pulled from the loom. Pull and stretch all of the bands into place.

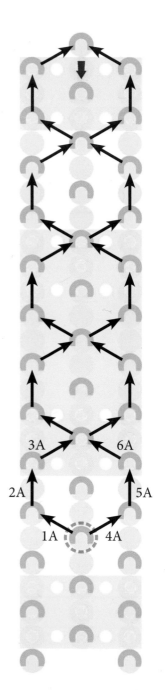

Rainbow Bloom Charm
Advanced

Date First Made:

7	**7**	**6**
A	**B**	**C**

PLACING THE BANDS

Step 1: Turn the loom so that the red arrow is pointing away from you. This design will only use a small section of the loom, so the diagrams show just the bottom section of the loom.

Step 2: Place bands 1 thru 3.

Step 3: Place bands 4 thru 6.

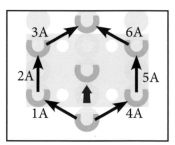

Step 4: Place bands 1 thru 6.

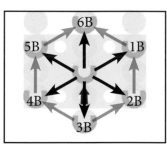

Step 5: Place bands 1 thru 3.

Step 6: Place bands 4 thru 6.

Step 7: Place Cap Band 7.

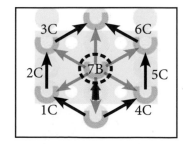

The Loomatic's Guide - www.LoomaticsGuide.com

Rainbow Bloom Charm
Advanced

LOOPING THE BANDS

Step 8: Turn the loom around so that the red arrow is pointing toward you.

Step 9: Loop bands 1 thru 6 as shown in the diagram on the right.

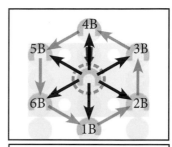

Step 10: Loop bands 1 thru 3.

Step 11: Loop bands 4 thru 6.

Step 12: Turn the loom around so the red arrow is pointing away from you.

Step 12: Lift the two "C" colored bands over the top of the center pin and place behind it. Lift the one on the right first, then the one on the left. See the two photos to the right.

Step 13: Tie off with an "A" colored band and pull into a slip knot.

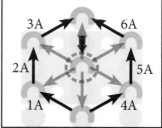

Lift these two red "C" bands over the top of the center pin.

Watch a short clip on how to finish the Rainbow Bloom Charm.

rbcfinish

The red "C" bands have been moved over the top and behind the center pin.

Carnation Bracelet
Advanced
Submitted by Ally Aufman
Wexford, PA

Date First Made:

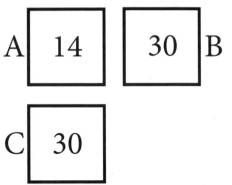

A 14   30 B

C 30

PLACING THE BANDS

Step 1: Turn the loom so that the red arrow is pointing away from you.

Step 2: Place bands 1 thru 12.

Step 3: Repeat the pattern 1 thru 12 to the end of the loom.

Things to try

Suggested colors:

A (Green)
B (White)
C (Pink)

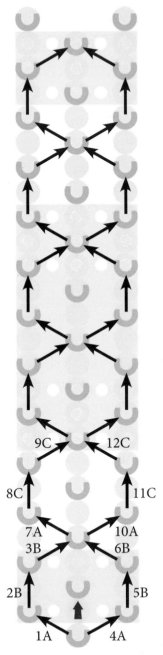

Carnation Bracelet
Advanced

PLACING THE BANDS

Step 4: Place bands 1 thru 12 as shown in the diagram below.

Step 5: Repeat the pattern 1 thru 12 to the end of the loom.

Step 6: Place an "A" colored Cap Band on the last pin as shown in the diagram. See "Making Cap Bands" on page 8.

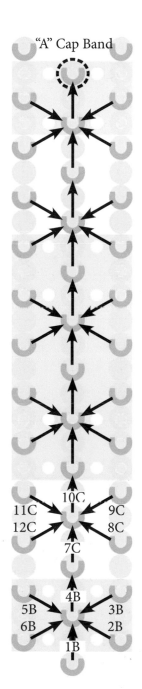

"A" Cap Band

11C 10C 9C
12C 8C
7C

5B 4B 3B
6B 2B
1B

Carnation Bracelet
Advanced

LOOPING THE BANDS

Step 7: Turn the loom around so that the red arrow is pointing toward you.

Step 8: Loop bands 1 thru 24.

Step 9: Repeat the pattern 1 thru 24 to the end of the loom.

Step 10: Tie off with an "A" colored band and go to "Finishing Your Bracelet" on page 12.

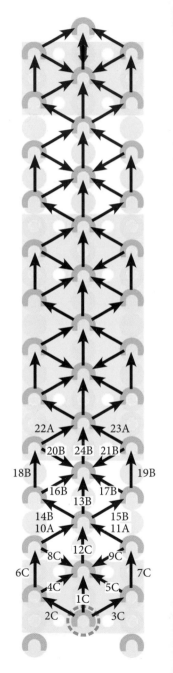

Bird of Paradise Bracelet
Advanced

Date First Made:

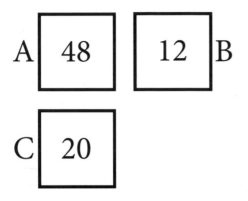

A	48

12	B

C	20

PLACING THE BANDS

Step 1: Convert the loom from an "offset" to a "rectangle" configuration. To learn how to do this, see "Loom Configurations" on page 182.

Step 2: Turn the loom so that the red arrow is pointing away from you.

Step 3: Place bands 1 thru 12.

Step 4: Place bands 13 thru 24.

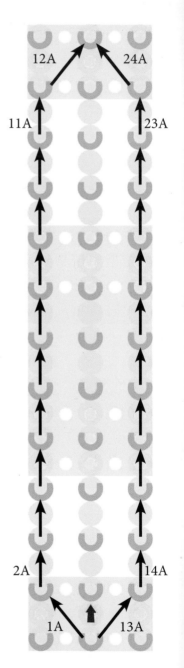

Bird of Paradise Bracelet
Advanced

PLACING THE BANDS

Step 5: Place band 1 as shown in the diagram below.

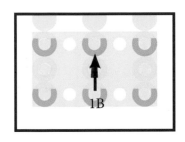

Step 6: Place bands 1 thru 5 as shown in the diagram to the right.

Step 7: Repeat the pattern 1 thru 5 to the next to last pin on the loom.

Step 8: Place bands 1, 2 and 3 at the end of the loom as shown in the diagram.

Step 9: Place an "A" colored Cap Band on the last pin as shown in the diagram. See "Making Cap Bands" on page 8.

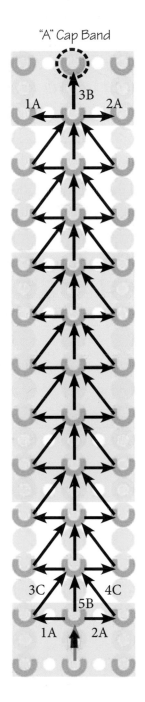

"A" Cap Band

Bird of Paradise Bracelet
Advanced

LOOPING THE BANDS

Step 10: Turn the loom around so that the red arrow is pointing toward you.

Step 11: On Row 1, loop bands 1 thru 3.

Step 12: On Row 2, loop bands 1 thru 7. The pattern is shown in the diagram to the right and is also shown below.

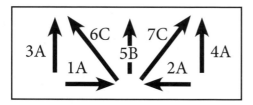

Step 13: On Rows 3 thru 11, repeat the pattern used on Row 2.

Step 14: On Row 12, loop bands 1 thru 5 as shown in the diagram to the right.

Step 15: Tie off with an "A" colored band and go to "Finishing Your Bracelet" on page 12.

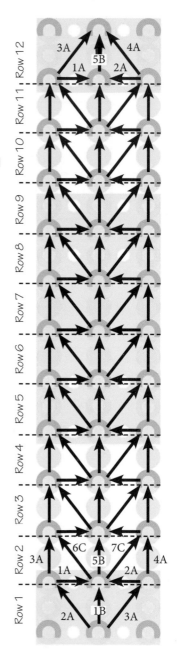

Delta Wing Bracelet
Advanced

Date First Made:

deltawing

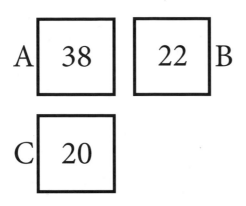

| A | 38 | | 22 | B |

| C | 20 |

PLACING THE BANDS

Step 1: Convert the loom from an "offset" to a "rectangle" configuration.

Step 2: Turn the loom so that the red arrow is pointing away from you.

Step 3: Place bands 1 thru 3 as shown in the diagram below.

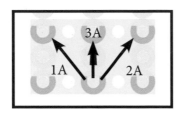

Step 4: Place bands 1 thru 14 as shown in the diagram to the right.

Step 5: Repeat the pattern 1 thru 14 four more times. See the diagram to the right for placing the last row of bands, 1 thru 5.

Step 6: Place an "A" colored Cap Band on the last pin as shown in the diagram.

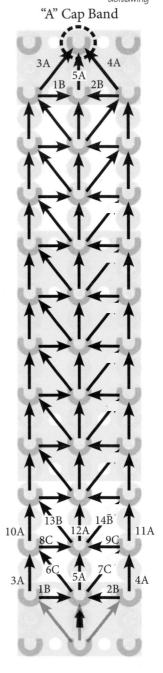

"A" Cap Band

Delta Wing Bracelet
Advanced

LOOPING THE BANDS

Step 7: Turn the loom around so that the red arrow is pointing toward you.

Step 8: Loop bands 1 thru 3 as shown in the diagram below.

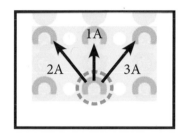

Step 9: Loop bands 1 thru 14 as shown in the diagram to the right.

Step 10: Repeat the pattern 1 thru 14 four more times.

Step 11: Loop bands 1 thru 5 at the end of the loom. See the diagram to the right.

Step 12: Tie off with an "A" colored band and go to "Finishing Your Bracelet" on page 12.

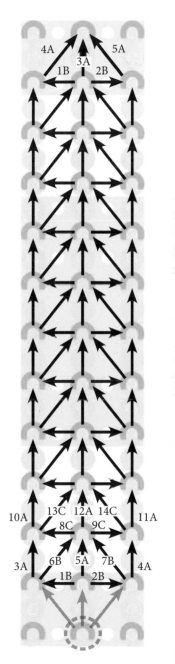

Totem Pole Bracelet
Advanced

Date First Made:

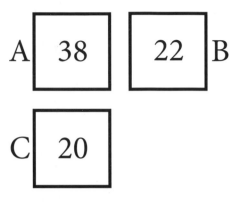

A 38   22 B

C 20

PLACING THE BANDS

Step 1: Convert the loom from an "offset" to a "rectangle" configuration. To learn how to do this, see "Loom Configurations" on page 182.

Step 2: Turn the loom so that the red arrow is pointing away from you.

Step 3: Place bands 1 thru 12.

Step 4: Place bands 13 thru 24.

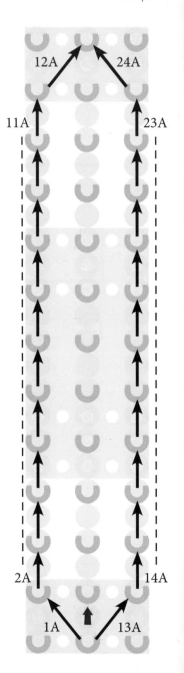

Totem Pole Bracelet
Advanced

PLACING THE BANDS

Step 5: Place bands 1 thru 3 as shown in the diagram below.

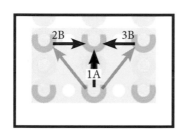

Step 6: Place bands 1 thru 10 as shown in the diagram to the right. This pattern is also shown below.

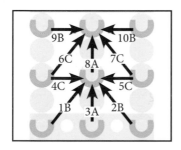

Step 7: Repeat the 1 thru 10 pattern 4 more times.

Step 8: Place the band labeled 1A on the diagram at the end of the loom.

Step 9: Place an "A" colored Cap Band on the last pin as shown in the diagram. See "Making Cap Bands" on page 8.

"A" Cap Band

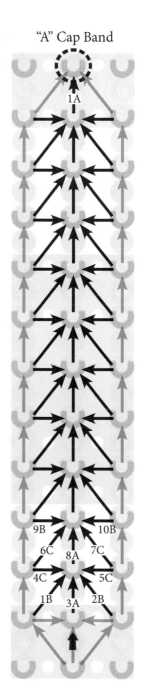

Totem Pole Bracelet
Advanced

LOOPING THE BANDS

Step 10: Turn the loom around so that the red arrow is pointing toward you.

Step 11: Loop the bands 1 thru 5 as shown in the diagram below.

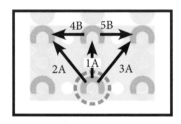

Step 12: Loop bands 1 thru 14 as shown in the diagram to the right and also below.

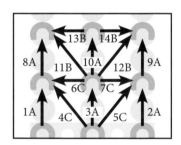

Step 13: Repeat the pattern 1 thru 14 four more times.

Step 14: Loop bands 1 thru 3 at the end of the loom as shown in the diagram to the right.

Step 15: Tie off with an "A" colored band and go to "Finishing Your Bracelet" on page 12.

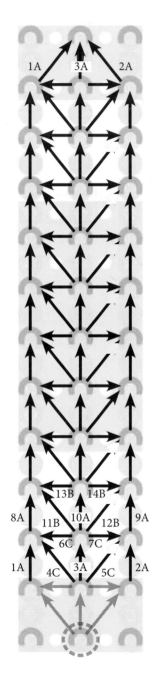

Fen's Fantastic Bracelet

Advanced
Named in honor of Choon's
wife, Fen Chan

Date First Made:

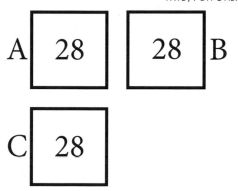

A | 28

28 | B

C | 28

PLACING THE BANDS

Step 1: Turn the loom so that the red arrow is pointing away from you.

Step 2: Place bands 1 thru 13.

Step 3: Place bands 14 thru 26.

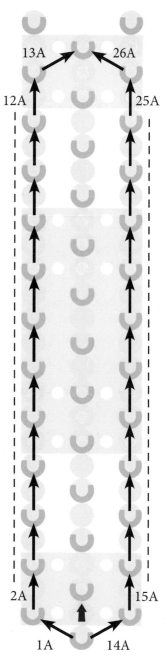

13A   26A

12A   25A

2A   15A

1A   14A

Fen's Fantastic Bracelet
Advanced

PLACING THE BANDS

Step 4: Place bands 1 thru 3 as shown in the diagram below.

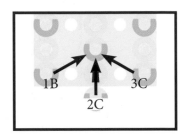

Step 5: Place bands 1 thru 10 as shown in the diagram to the right.

Step 6: Repeat the pattern 1 thru 10 to the end of the loom. Do not place bands 9 & 10 at the end of the loom as shown in the diagram.

Step 7: Place an "A" colored Cap Band on the last pin as shown in the diagram. See "Making Cap Bands" on page 8.

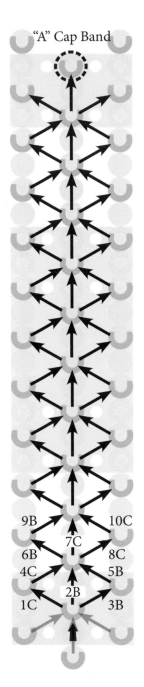

Fen's Fantastic Bracelet
Advanced

LOOPING THE BANDS

Step 8: Turn the loom around so that the red arrow is pointing toward you.

Step 9: Loop bands 1 thru 3 as shown in the diagram below.

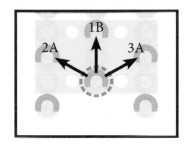

Step 10: Loop bands 1 thru 14 as shown in the diagram to the right.

Step 11: Repeat the pattern 1 thru 14 four more times.

Step 12: Loop bands 1 thru 9 as shown at the top of the diagram.

Step 13: Tie off with an "A" colored band and go to "Finishing Your Bracelet" on page 12.

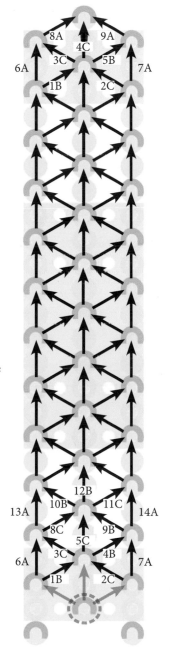

Feather Bracelet
Advanced

Date First Made:

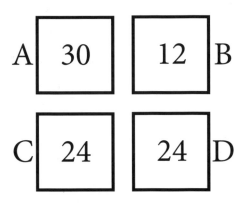

A	30	12	B
C	24	24	D

PLACING THE BANDS

Step 1: Convert the loom from an "offset" to a "rectangle" configuration. To learn how to do this, see "Loom Configurations" on page 182.

Step 2: Turn the loom so that the red arrow is pointing away from you.

Step 3: Place bands 1 thru 14.

Step 4: Place bands 15 thru 28.

Step 5: Push the bands all the way down on the pins.

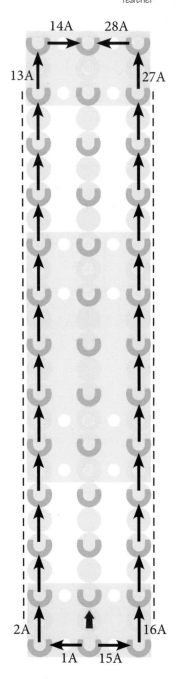

Feather Bracelet
Advanced

PLACING THE BANDS

Step 6: Place bands 1 thru 3.

Step 7: Repeat the pattern 1 thru 3 to the end of the loom.

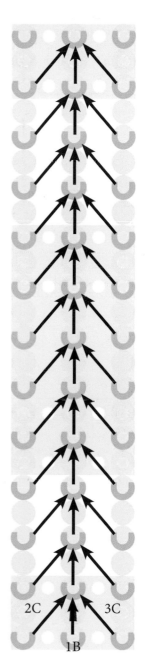

Feather Bracelet
Advanced

PLACING THE BANDS

Step 8: Place bands 1 and 2.

Step 9: Repeat 1 and 2 pattern to the end of the loom as shown.

Step 10: Place an "A" colored Cap Band as shown.

Step 11: Push all bands down onto the pins. Looping this design is difficult and will take patience. Make sure you follow the pattern closely.

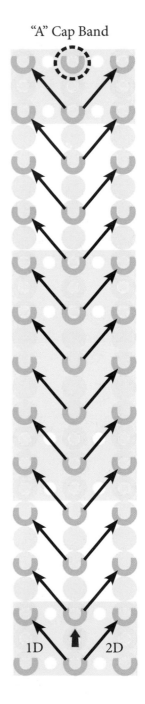

"A" Cap Band

1D   2D

Feather Bracelet
Advanced

LOOPING THE BANDS

Step 12: Turn the loom around so that the red arrow is pointing toward you.

Step 13: Starting on Row 1 (see diagram to the right), loop bands 1 thru 9 as shown below.

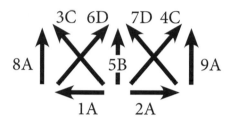

Step 14: Starting on Row 2 (see diagram to the right), loop bands 1 thru 7 as shown below. Repeat this pattern for Row 3 thru Row 11.

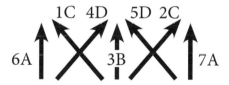

Step 15: Starting on Row 12 (see diagram to the right), loop bands 1 thru 9 as shown below.

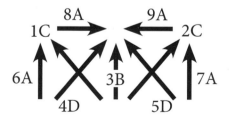

Step 16: Tie off with an "A" colored band and go to "Finishing Your Bracelet" on page 12.

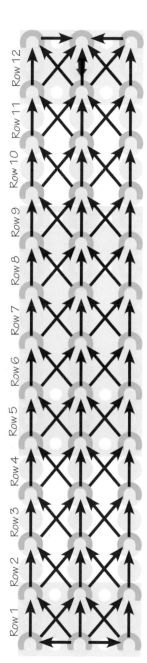

Confetti Criss-Cross
Advanced
Submitted by Kylee Crawford
Reno, NV

crisscross

Date First Made:

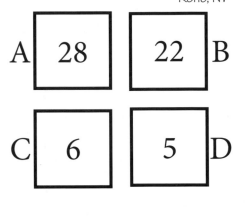

A **28**	**22** B
C **6**	**5** D

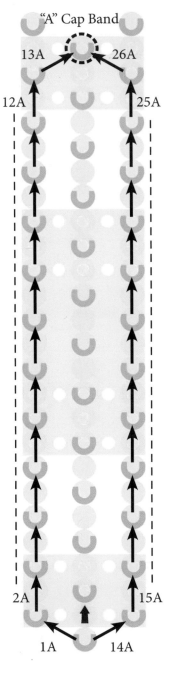

PLACING THE BANDS

Step 1: Turn the loom so that the red arrow is pointing away from you.

Step 2: Place bands 1 thru 13.

Step 3: Place bands 14 thru 26.

Step 4: Place an "A" colored Cap Band on the last pin as shown in the diagram. See "Making Cap Bands" on page 8.

Confetti Criss-Cross Bracelet
Advanced

PLACING THE BANDS

Step 5: Place bands 1 thru 11. Notice how these bands are stretched over 3 pins to form a triangle.

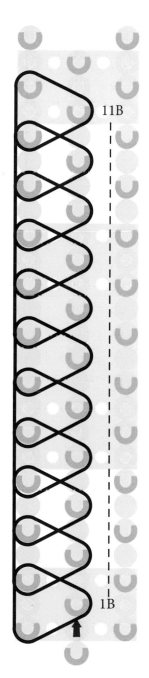

11B

1B

Confetti Criss-Cross Bracelet
Advanced

PLACINGTHE BANDS

Step 6: Place bands 1 thru 11. Once again, these
are stretched over 3 pins to form a triangle.

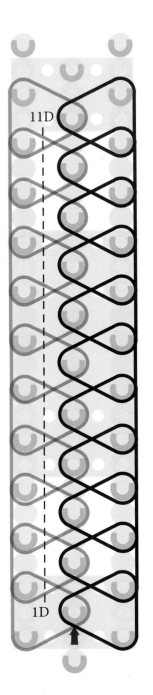

11D

1D

Confetti Criss-Cross Bracelet
Advanced

PLACING THE BANDS

Step 7: Place "double" Cap Bands 1 thru 11 alternating "C" and "D" colored bands. Or you can make a rainbow pattern, if you prefer, with the double Cap Bands.

A double Cap Band is a band looped 4 times around the pin instead of 2 times like a regular Cap Band.

The easiest way I have found to do this is to wrap a band around the twist end of a lip balm tube 4 times, and then put the lip balm tube over the pin and push the Cap Band onto the pin.

Making a double Cap Band.

doublecap

Another way is to just wrap a band around the pin 4 times like you would a pony tail, but this may be more difficult.

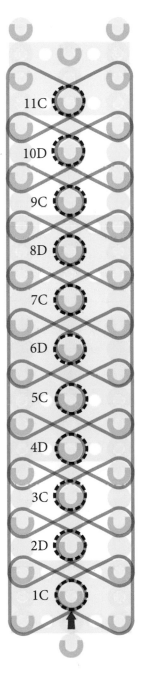

Confetti Criss-Cross Bracelet
Advanced

LOOPING THE BANDS

Step 8: Turn the loom around so that the red arrow is pointing toward you.

Step 9: Loop each of the triangle bands on the left side, bands 1 thru 11 in the figure. For clarity, the first band in the diagram is colored red.

To loop the triangle bands, reach inside of the double Cap Band, grab the triangle band, then stretch it over BOTH pins on the outside row of the loom. If done correctly, it will look like the photo below. Hold the Cap Band in place with your finger while looping.

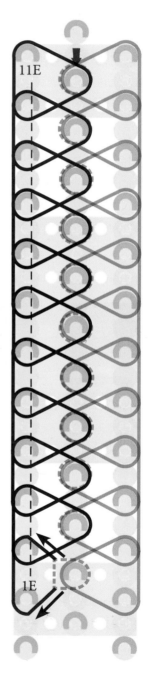

Notice how the triangle band is pulled through the green Cap Band and streched over both outer pins, right back over itself.

To watch this being done, scan the QR code.

ccc_triangles

Confetti Criss-Cross Bracelet
Advanced

LOOPING THE BANDS

Step 10: Repeat the same procedure on the right side of the loom for triangle bands 1 thru 11 in the figure to the right.

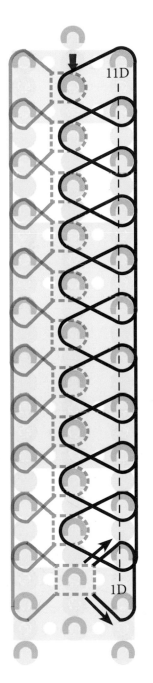

11D

1D

Confetti Criss-Cross Bracelet
Advanced

LOOPING THE BANDS

Step 11: Loop bands 1 thru 13.

Step 12: Loop bands 14 thru 26.

Step 13: Tie off with an "A" colored band and go to "Finishing Your Bracelet" on page 12.

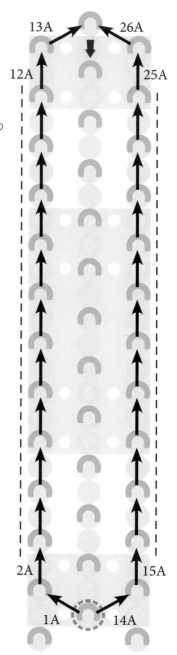

Hibiscus Bracelet
Advanced
Submitted by Madeline Grasso
Cummings, GA

hibiscus

Date First Made:

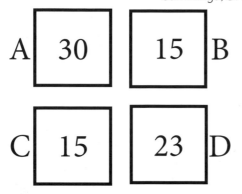

| A | 30 | 15 | B |
| C | 15 | 23 | D |

As seen on the TODAY
show 8/15/2013

PLACING THE BANDS

Step 1: Turn the loom so that the red arrow is pointing away from you.

Step 2: Place bands 1 thru 12 as shown in the diagram to the right.

Step 3: For the first petal you make, place a "D" colored Cap Band as shown on the diagram. For the remaining 4 petals, you will use the Cap Band that is on the first petal that you made. In the end, you will have 5 petals attached to the same Cap Band.

LOOPING THE BANDS

Step 4: Turn the loom so that the red arrow is pointing toward you.

Step 5: Loop bands 1 thru 12.

Step 6: Place a C-clip over the 10 & 12 bands and remove the petal from the loom. Set the petal aside for now. You will be adding more petals to it.

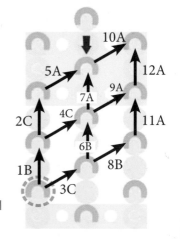

"D" Cap Band

Hibiscus Bracelet
Advanced

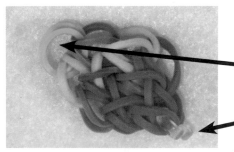

This is a photo of the first petal.

Notice the Cap Band. You will be adding 4 more petals to this Cap Band in the next step.

The C-clip is the tip of the petal.

Note: Each of the additional petal uses the same Cap Band as used on your 1st petal. (see photo)

Step 7: Repeat Steps 1 thru 6 four more times to add four more petals to the flower.

This will make a flower with 5 petals attached to the same Cap Band.

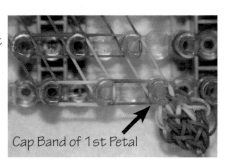

Cap Band of 1st Petal

Step 8: To make a bracelet with the Hibiscus flower, make a single chain with 11 "D" colored bands. Slide the petals of the Hibiscus flower apart and add its Cap Band as the 12th band in the single chain. (see photo)

Step 9: Loop the single chain and finish with a C-clip.

Step 10: Add 11 more "D" colored bands in a single chain to the other side of the Hibiscus flower. Complete the bracelet by connecting the two ends of the single chain bracelet together with the C-clip that was added in Step 9.

Note: For a larger wrist, you may need more than 22 bands in your single chain.

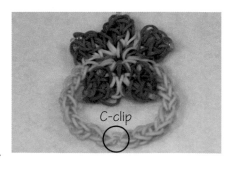

C-clip

Loom Configurations

There are four basic configurations for the Rainbow Loom: "Offset", "Rectangular", End-to-End, and Side-by-Side. The following explains the three configurations used in this book. To change the Rainbow Loom from one configuration to the other, use the base removal tool on the end of your hook to pry the turquise base plates from the loom. When you reassemble the loom, make sure that the base plates are pressed firmly back into place.

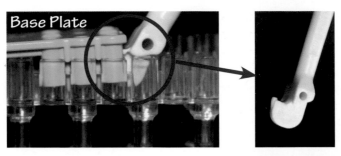

Base Plate

Offset Configuration

Out of the box, your Rainbow Loom comes in the "Offset" configuration as shown in the photo to the right. Notice how the middle row of pins is offset one half pin forward from the outside two rows of pins.

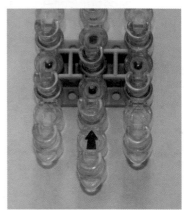

Rectangular Configuration

The "Rectangular" configuration also known as the squared off configuration is shown to the right. Notice how all of the rows of pins line up.

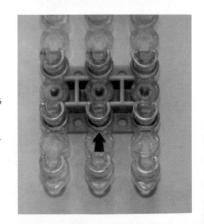

End-to-End Configuration

The majority of the bracelet patterns in this book, if made on one loom, will require an extension to fit comfortably around an adult wrist. Two Rainbow Looms can be configured End-to-End to create a full length bracelet that will wrap fully around any wrist! You can adjust the size of the bracelet by determining how many pins you will need to use.

The information below will serve as a rough guideline for your requirements:

13 pins on the loom = 4 inches or ~10cm of bracelet
20 pins on the loom = 6 inches or ~15cm of bracelet
26 pins on the loom = 8 inches or ~20cm of bracelet

In this example, we will show you how to set two looms in the End-to-End/ Offset configuration. The End-to-End/Rectangular configuration steps are basically the same.

Step 1: Place two looms, upside-down, side-by-side, in front of you, with the arrows pointing in the same direction.

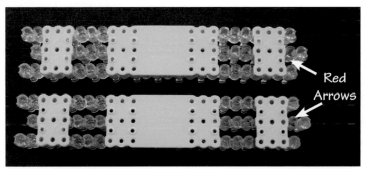

Red Arrows

Step 2: Use the base plate tool on the end of the hook to pry one small base plate from one loom and one small base plate and a large base plate from the other as shown below. Set these base plates aside.

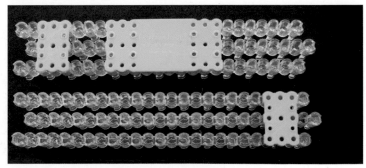

Step 4: Place the looms end-to end with a small gap between them.

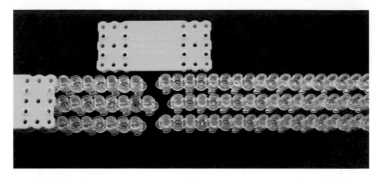

Step 5: Center the large base over the gap between the two looms, adjust, and press the large base plate firmly into place.

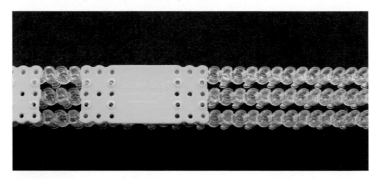

Step 6: Place the two small base plates on the second loom, roughly, 3 to 4 of the open holes apart, and press firmly into place.

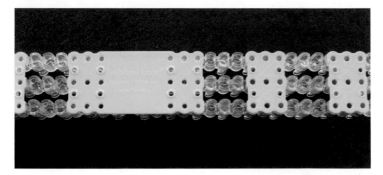

Blank Design Templates

I used blank design templates like these to prepare the instructions for this book. Now it's your turn! Here are some blank templates for you to design your own creations!

You may photocopy the templates if you like, but please don't photocopy the instructions in the book.

If you come up with some neat designs, I'd love to see them. If you want it published in our next book, you will find instructions on our website www.loomaticsguide.com on how to submit designs.

Have fun being creative!

Offset Configuration

Offset Configuration

Rectangular Configuration

Acknowledgements

Design Submissions
Ally Auffman, Wexford, PA
Fen Chan, Novi, MI
Kylee Crawford, Reno, NV Learning Express
Maddie Grasso, Cummings, GA
Lori LaRosa, Marlton, NJ of LL Beads4U
Lyndsey West, Reno, NV Learning Express
Danielle Wilhelm, Sylvania, OH Learning Express

Graphics & Photography
Logan Peterson, Reno, NV
Wade Peterson, Reno, NV

Website
Carol Villar, Reno, NV

Printing
The Crew at DynaGraphics, Reno, NV: Spencer, Alan, Alfred, Cindy, Linda, & Rich

Support
Kylee Crawford, Reno, NV
Jan Fowler, Redmond, WA
Celine Kirchman, Reno, NV
Carter Peterson, Reno, NV

Our parents Clare Peterson, Hal & Judy Martin and Nancy Martin

We would like to thank the crew at Learning Express Toys of Reno, NV for all of their support!

South Reno: Brendan D, Celine K, Tyler O, Maddy P, Sheri P, Lyndsey W, Teresa W,

Northwest Reno: Ashley B, Kylee C, Ben H, Dawn K, Brittany M, Amanda M, Sarah Y

Inspiration
Colleen Hendon, Roseville, CA and her father, Bob Clifford, "Follow Your Bliss"
Linda Kranz, Flagstaff, AZ, "Find Your Passion. Do what you love!"
David Horvath and Sun-Min Kim